Python Data

Mastering Python for Beginners.
A Step-by-Step Guide for Beginners
(2022 Crash Course for All)

Dennis Field

Table of Contents

Python Data Science

Introduction

There are numerous options available to a business when it comes to the locations and sources from which it can collect data. Many businesses will hire data scientists to assist them in gathering information from sources such as social media, sensors, digital videos, and pictures, purchased transactions from their customers, and even surveys that the customers may have completed.

Because there are so many sources from which the company can obtain the information they seek, it won't take much research before the company is inundated with all of the presented data. There is simply so much data available, which is fantastic, but we must ensure that we know the proper steps to handle the information and learn what is available, rather than simply collecting the data and calling it good.

A large part of Data Science is the analysis that you will perform on all of the data that comes in. All of this enables us to pool a wide range of professional skills in order to handle and apply that information. Yes, it will include searching for the information, so don't forget about it or skip over it, but it can also come in and help with understanding the information. To accomplish all of this, we need a few skills to come together, either in one person or within a team, to make Data Science useful. Some of the things that Data Science and the information we collect will be able to assist us with are as follows.

- reducing the number of costs that the company must deal with
- Assisting in the launch of a brand-new service or product and knowing it will be successful.
- To aid in determining the effectiveness of a new marketing campaign.
- To assist in reaching out to various demographics along the way.
- To ensure that we can enter and succeed in a new market.

Of course, this is not an exhaustive list, and knowing the right steps to take and all of the benefits that come with working in Data Science can help us see some improvements and help the business grow. You can use Data Science to help your business succeed no matter what products or services you sell, where you are located, or what industry you are in.

It can be difficult for businesses to see how Data Science can help them improve. We could conclude that this is all a bunch of nonsense, or that only a few companies have had success with it. However, a plethora of companies, including household names such as Amazon, Visa, and Google, can benefit from this type of information. While your company may or may not be on the same level as those three, you can still put Data Science to work for you, improving what you can offer on the market, how you can help customers, and so much more.

It is important to note that Data Science is already taking over the world and assisting businesses in a variety of ways. For example, it demonstrates to businesses the best way to grow, how to reach their customers in the most effective and efficient way, how to find new sources of value, and much more. It often depends on the company's overall goal for using this Data Science process to determine what they will get out of it.

With all of the benefits that come with using this Data Science process, and all of the big-name companies that are jumping on board and attempting to gain some of the knowledge and benefits as well, we need to look at the Data Science life cycle, and the steps that it takes to make this project a huge success. Let's take a look at some of the things we need to know about the data life cycle so we can understand the fundamentals of what needs to happen to see success with Data Science.

The discovery of data

The first step we'll see with this life cycle is the idea that businesses need to get out there and find the information they want to use. This is the stage at which we will search a variety of sources for the information we require. Sometimes the data will be structured, such as in text format, but other times it will be unstructured, such as videos and images.

There are times when the data we find is delivered to us in the form of a relational database system.

These are some of the more traditional methods for gathering information, but it is also possible for an organisation to investigate other options. For example, many businesses are turning to social media to help them reach their customers and gain a better understanding of their mindsets and purchasing decisions.

Often, this phase will involve us starting with a big question that we want answered and then searching for the data, either in the first place or, if we already have the data, searching through the information that we have already gathered. This makes it easier for us to sift through all of that data and find the insights we seek.

Getting the information ready

After we have spent some time searching through all of the different sources for the information that we require, it is time to consider how we can use data, and data preparation will assist us in this. This phase includes a few steps; basically, we will convert the information from all of those different sources into one common format so that they can work together, and an algorithm that we choose later will be able to handle the data without errors or mistakes.

This is a more involved process, but it is where the data scientist will begin collecting clean subsets of data and then insert the defaults and parameters that are required for you. In some cases, the methods you employ will be more complex, such as identifying some of the values that are missing from the data, and so on.

Another thing you should do while you're here is clean up the data. This is critical when collecting data from multiple sources because it ensures that the data is consistent and that the algorithm you choose will be able to read it all later. You also want to ensure that no information is missing, that duplicate values have been removed, and that nothing else has been discovered within the set of data you want to work with that will reduce the accuracy of the model you are attempting to create.

After you have gone through and cleaned off the data you want to use, the next step is to integrate it and then create our conclusion based on the set of data for the analysis. This analysis will entail taking the data and then merging two or more tables that contain the same objects but different information. It can also include the aggregation process, which is when we summarise the various fields found in the table as we go through the process.

During this whole process, the goal is for us to explore and then come up with an understanding of the patterns, as well as the values, that are going to show up in the data set that we are working with. This will take some time and patience, but it will ensure that any mathematical models we work with later make sense and work the way we want them to.

Mathematical models

When working with Data Science, all of the projects you will want to work on will require the use of mathematical models to help them get everything done. These are models that we can plan ahead of time, and then the data scientist will build them to help suit the needs of the business or the question that they want answered.

In some cases, it is possible to complete these models by collaborating with a few different areas of mathematics, such as linear regression, statistics, and logistics.

To get all of this done, we must also ensure that we are employing the appropriate tools and methods. Some of the statistical computing tools included with R can be useful, as can working with other advanced analytical tools such as SQL and Python, as well as any visualisation tool required to ensure the data makes sense.

Also, we must ensure that we are getting satisfactory results from all of our efforts, which may necessitate the use of more than one algorithm or model to achieve this. In this case, the data scientist must go through the data and create a group of models that can work together to go through the data and answer any questions that the business has.

After measuring out the models that they want to use, the data scientist can revise some of the parameters that are already in place and fine-tune them as they go through the next round of modelling. This process will take several rounds to complete because you will need to test it more than once to ensure that it will work the way you want it to.

Putting it all together

We've had a chance to prepare the data the way it needs to be prepared, and we've been able to build some of the models that we want to use. With this in mind, it is time to work with the models to get them to produce the types of results that are required. It is possible that there will be a few discrepancies, depending on the data you have and the model you choose, and you may have to go through a few levels of troubleshooting to deal with the process, but this is normal. Most data scientists must make changes to their models as they progress through the process before arriving at the best solution for them.

Of course, in order to see how the model will perform in the real world, we must first test it. This is the best way to see what will happen when the model is in use, rather than just a theory.

You can try out a new algorithm with it as well to see if one type is a better option than any of the others. This is sometimes the point at which we decide to include more than one algorithm to handle our data needs.

The significance of communication

While we're going through the data life cycle, we should take a moment to discuss how important communication can be throughout the process. A good data scientist, or a good team of data scientists, will not only work with algorithms and numbers; they will also handle the communication that must take place. Someone on the business end, such as marketers and key decision-makers, will need to be able to read through this information, and the data scientist must be able to communicate in an understandable manner.

One of the critical steps in the data life cycle will be communicating what has been discovered within the data and through the various algorithms used. During this stage, the professional will be able to communicate with the various teams that are present, and they must be skilled enough to communicate and share their findings clearly and concisely.

Many different people will require this information, and not all of them will be data scientists or people who understand some of the technical aspects that are involved. The data scientist must still share this information to ensure that these key decision-makers understand the information and the insights discovered in the data. The information can then be used by decision-makers to determine which direction to take their company.

One thing to keep in mind here is that a data scientist must ensure that they are communicating in a variety of ways. This can often include both the written and spoken word, so prepare to work on some public speaking and interpersonal skills to get things done.

However, written and spoken words will not be the only places where the data scientist will need to be able to communicate. For example, the final component of Data Science and its lifecycle is some kind of visualisation of the information and insights found in all of that data. These visualisations can take all of the numbers and data and turn it into an image, such as a bar chart, a graph, a pie chart, or some other method or image.

This is useful because it can take a large amount of information and condense it into a format that we can quickly scan and understand. Instead of having to go through all of the different pieces of information and read through all of the data, we can use these images to help us see and understand what is going on, what relationships showed up for each part, and so much more.

The data life cycle is critical for understanding what is in all of that data that you have accumulated over time. Companies can collect more data than ever before, but they must know how to convert it into a usable format. This is often easier said than done, but by working with the data life cycle that we discussed earlier, you will be able to not only collect all of the data but also use it to make some good business decisions.

Chapter 1: History of Data Science

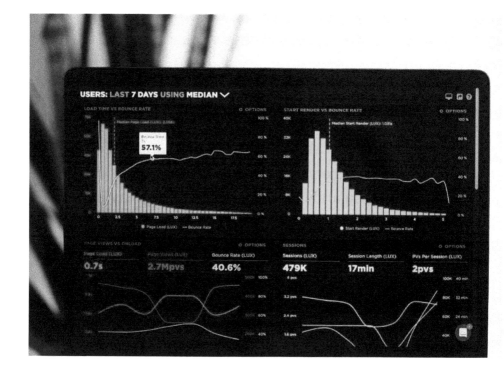

Deep learning can be traced back to 1943 when Warren McCulloch and Walter Pitts published a paper proposing the concept of an Artificial Neuron (AN) to mimic the thought process. This Artificial Neuron was based on the biological neuron's characteristic of being either fully active to stimulation or not at all. This biological neuron behaviour was observed in brain microelectrode readings.

As the first implementation of the perceptron algorithm, Frank and Rosenblatt presented the Mark I Perceptron Machine in 1957. The goal was to create an agent that could learn by mimicking the operation of a biological neuron. This perceptron was a supervised binary linear classifier with weights that could be adjusted.

This formula provided classification results for each input and output pair based on $f(x)$, the function's predicted value/output.

Widrow and Hoff stacked these perceptrons in 1960 and created ADALINE, a three-layered (input layer, hidden layer, output layer), fully connected, feed-forward architecture for classification.

Henry J. Kelley introduced a continuous back propagation model in 1960, which is still used in the model's learning weights today.

Stuart Dreyfus introduced a simpler version of backpropagation based on the chain rule in 1962, but these methods were inefficient. Backpropagation, which is now used in models, was introduced in the 1980s.

Fukushima created the Neocognitron, a multi-layered Convolutional Neural Network architecture that could learn to recognise patterns in images, in 1979. The network was similar to but not identical to modern architectures. It also enabled the user to manually adjust the weight of specific connections. Many Neocognitron concepts are still in use. Perceptrons' layered connections can be used to build a variety of neural networks. The Selective Attention Model was able to distinguish and separate several patterns in the data.

Seppo Linnainmaa presented automatic differentiation in 1970, which used the chain rule to efficiently compute the derivative of a differentiable composite function. Later in 1986, its application resulted in the backpropagation of errors in multilayer perceptrons. Geoff Hinton, Williams, and Rumelhart presented a paper demonstrating that backpropagation in neural networks provides interesting distribution representations at this time. Yann LeCun, the current Director of AI Research, was born in 1989.

At Bell Labs, Facebook provided the first practical demonstration of backpropagation in Convolutional Neural Networks to read handwritten digits.

Deep neural networks were unable to train well even with backpropagation.

Vapnik and Cortes pioneered the use of support vector machines for data-regression and classification in 1995. Schmidhuber and Hochreiter proposed Long Short Term Memory (LSTM) for recurrent neural networks in 1997.

Throughout these years, a significant impediment was computed, but in 1999, computers began to become faster at processing data, and Graphical Processing Units (GPUs) were introduced. This greatly increased compute power.

Hinton and Salakhutdinov presented a paper in 2006 that re-energized deep learning research. This was the first time a proper 10-layer Convolutional Neural Network was properly trained. Instead of using backpropagation to train

10 layers, they devised an unsupervised pre-training scheme called Restricted Boltzmann Machine. This was a two-step training procedure. In the first step, an unsupervised objective was used to train each layer of the network. The layers were stacked together for backpropagation in the second step.

Later that year, Fei-Fei Li, a Stanford University professor, launched ImageNet, a large visual database designed for visual object recognition research that contains over 14 million hand-annotated images of 20,000 different object categories. This gave neural networks a significant advantage because data of this order allowed neural networks to be trained and achieve good results.

When Microsoft presented a paper on speech recognition in 2010, neural networks drew a lot of attention from the research community because they outperformed other Machine Learning tools like SVMs and kernels. They achieved significant improvements by incorporating neural networks into the GMM and HMM frameworks.

A paper published in 2012 by Krizhevsky, Sutskever, and Hinton demonstrated that deep learning can achieve significant improvements in the visual recognition domain. In visual recognition tasks, their model, AlexNet, outperformed all other traditional computer vision methods and won several international competitions. Since then, the field has exploded, and several network architectures and ideas, such as GANs, have been introduced.

Chapter 2: Working with Python for Data Science

Programming languages enable us to apply our theoretical knowledge to something that could occur. Data Science, which typically requires a large amount of data to make things happen, will, by definition, make use of programming languages to organise the data for subsequent steps in model development. So, let's get started learning Python for a better understanding of the subject.

What is the significance of Python?

To make this problem more concrete, imagine we have a small partner named Estella. She recently graduated from the math department and landed a job in data science. On her first day of work, she was ecstatic and eager to learn about this new industry. But she soon discovered a major problem: the data required to process the work is stored on remote servers, some of which are traditional relational databases and others are Hadoop clusters. In contrast to Windows, which is mostly used on desktop computers, Linux-like systems are used on remote servers. Estella is unfamiliar with this operating system because it lacks the familiar graphical interface. All operations, including the most basic file reading, must be programmed by the user.

As a result, Estella is eager to discover a programming language that is simple to write, simple to learn, and simple to use.

Worse, familiar data modelling software, such as SPSS and MATLAB, cannot be used in the new working environment. Estella, on the other hand, frequently employs some of the software's basic algorithms in her daily work, such as linear regression and logical regression. As a result, she hopes that the programming language she discovers will also include an easy-to-use library of algorithms, and, of course, it is preferable if it is free.

The entire process is reminiscent of Estella's favourite game, table tennis. The assumption is sent to the data as a "ball," and then the adjustment is made based on the data's "return ball," and the preceding actions are repeated. As a result, Estella added one more request to her list: the programming language can be modified and used at any time without requiring compilation. It's preferable to have an immediate response command window so she can quickly validate her ideas.

Estella was overjoyed when she discovered Python, an IT tool that met all of her requirements, after conducting extensive research.

I hope you now have a good understanding of why programming languages are important in data science. In the following sections, we will go over the language and its basic functions in great detail.

What exactly is Python?

Python is a computer programming language that is both object-oriented and interpretive. It has a simple syntax and a collection of standard libraries with complete functions that can easily accomplish many common tasks. When it comes to Python, its origins are also fascinating. During the 1989 Christmas holidays, Dutch programmer Guido van Rossum stayed at home and did nothing. So, in order to pass the "boring" time, he created the first version of Python.

Python is a popular programming language. According to GitHub, an opensource community, it has been one of the most popular programming languages in the last ten years, surpassing traditional C, C++ languages, and C#, which is widely used in Windows systems. Estella believes Python is a programming language specifically designed for non-professional programmers after using it for a while.

Its grammatical structure is very concise, encouraging everyone to write as much easy-to-understand code as possible while writing as little code as possible.

Python has a large number of standard libraries as well as third-party libraries. Estella bases her application on these existing programmes, which allows her to achieve twice the results with half the effort and accelerate the development process.

Python, on the other hand, can be shipped across platforms. Estella, for example, frequently writes Python code on their familiar Windows system and then deploys the developed programme to the Linux system's server. To summarise, Python is studious and simple to use.

Python's Role in Data Science

Estella can do many interesting things after learning Python as a programming language, such as writing a web crawler, collecting data from the Internet, creating a task scheduling system, update the model on a regular basis, and so on.

Estella uses Python for Data Science applications in the following ways:

Cleaning of Data

Estella will first perform preliminary processing on the data after obtaining the original data, such as unifying the case of the string, correcting incorrect data, and so on. This is also known as "cleaning up" "dirty" data to make it more suitable for analysis. Estella can easily complete this step of work using Python and its third-party library pandas.

Visualization of Data

Estella displays data graphically using Matplotlib. Estella can get the first intuitive feeling of the data from the graph and enlighten the thinking before extracting the features. Information can be clearly and effectively conveyed and communicated with the help of graphics when communicating with colleagues in other departments, so those insights can be put on paper.

Extraction of Characteristics

In this step, Richard typically associates relevant data stored in various locations, such as integrating basic customer information and customer shopping information via customer ID. The data is then transformed and the variables useful for modelling are extracted.

These variables are referred to as features. Estella will use Python's NumPy, SciPy, pandas, and PySpark in this process.

Model Construction

Almost all of the commonly used basic algorithms are covered by the open-source libraries sci-kit-learn, StatsModels, Spark ML, and TensorFlow.

Estella can easily build the basic algorithms together and create the model she wants based on these algorithm bases and the data characteristics and algorithm assumptions. The four items listed above are also the four core steps in Data Science.

It's no surprise that Estella, like the majority of data scientists, chose Python as a tool to complete his work.

Structure of Python Engineering

The engineering structure of Python projects is discussed in this section.

This section of the beginner's content may be more abstract. If readers find the following text difficult to understand, they can skip ahead to the next section, which will not affect their reading of the remaining chapters in this book.

Assume Estella has written some scripts and saved them in a file directory. As a reader, you may hope to reuse previous code when creating a new project, such as when using a third-party library such as NumPy. How should this be accomplished? The solution is to include " in your init .py file ""aggressive." Take a look at the following example.

To begin, make a mini project directory that contains two subdirectories: components and tests. There are, however, two Python scripts under components: counter.py and selecter.py.

The wordCount function is defined in the counter.py script, and the getFrequentItem function is defined in the selecter.py script.

This function is dependent on the above-mentioned wordCount function, so import it at the start of the script with the following command:

[command for user input] counter [to obtain] function

tests/test selector.py is the program's entry point, that is, the script that will be run directly and will call the getFrequentItem function. Similarly, at the start of this script, import getFrequentItem.

[command for user input] [to obtain] frequency function

If you run the programme now with the "Python test selector.py" command, you will get the following error message:

error: does not exist as a module

Because Python does not consider the directory mini-project to be a usable library, the import failed. Simply create an empty init .py file in each directory to fix this bug.

Python's library is essentially a directory containing init .py files.

The properties and methods of this library are defined in init .py. We import the init .py file when we use the import command to import a library. Under normal circumstances, there is no need to define anything in it; just an empty file is required, and Python will process it automatically using the default settings.

However, if this file is missing, Python will not recognise the corresponding directory as a third-party library, and we will be unable to import and use it.

It's also worth noting that when importing a library, you must ensure that the corresponding directory is visible in the system path. To put it another way, the corresponding library directory is located under" ys.path". If this is not the case, the corresponding path must be added to "sys. path."

We have now given a thorough introduction to Python and why it is a viable option for Data Science. In the following chapter, we'll go over Python operations in greater depth. This knowledge will be useful in future Data Science projects. So, what are you waiting for? Let's get started.

Chapter 3: How Machine Learning Fits with Data Science

The following topic that we need to look at is Machine Learning and how it comes into play when working with Data Science, as well as all of the cool things that we can do with this topic. Machine learning can undoubtedly be an important part of the Data Science process if used correctly.

Remember that part of Data Science is working on data analysis as we go through this process. This allows us to take a large amount of data that we have gathered along the way and actually see the insights and predictions that are contained within it. To make this happen, we need to be able to build models that can sort through all of the data, find hidden patterns, and provide us with insights.

To define these models and ensure that they work as intended, we need a variety of good algorithms in place, and this is where Machine Learning will come into play quite a bit. You will discover that with the help of Machine Learning and the various algorithms available in Machine Learning, we can create models that can go through any type of data we have, large or small, and provide us with the answers that we require here.

Machine learning is a process that can be used to train the system or machine with which we are working to think like humans. This enables the algorithm to search for hidden patterns in the same way that a human would, but much faster and more efficiently than any human could do manually.

Consider how difficult it would be to do this manually for any human, or even a group of people attempting to sort through all of that data. It could take years for them to sift through all of that data and find the insights they require. And, given how quickly data is generated and collected, those predictions and insights would be worthless by the time we arrived at that point.

This process can be greatly aided by machine learning. It enables us to think through the data in order to uncover hidden patterns and insights that are relevant to our needs. We can learn how the process works and all of the steps required to make this happen for us with the right Machine Learning algorithm. With this in mind, it is time to take a closer look at Machine Learning and all of the components that we need to understand in order to make it work for us.

What exactly is Machine Learning?

The first thing we need to look at is the fundamentals of Machine Learning. Machine learning will be one of the artificial intelligence applications that can provide a system with the ability to learn on its own, without the assistance of a programmer telling the system what to do. The system can even go a step further and work to improve based on its own experience, all without the system being explicitly programmed in the process. Machine Learning will be done with a focus on the development of computer programmes that can access any data you have and then use that presented data to learn something new and how you want it to behave.

When it comes to using Machine Learning, there will be a variety of applications to consider. As we learn more about what Machine Learning can do, you may notice that it has been able to change and develop into something that programmers will enjoy working with more than ever before.

Machine Learning is the right option for you if you want to make your machine or system do a lot of the work on its own without you having to step in and programme every step.

When it comes to technology, we will discover that Machine Learning is quite unique and can add a level of fun to the coding that we do. There are already many companies in a variety of industries (which we will discuss in a moment) that will use Machine Learning and are reaping significant benefits from it.

There are numerous applications for Machine Learning, and it is amazing what we can accomplish with this type of artificial intelligence. When it comes to Machine Learning, some of the best methods to follow and focus our time on are as follows:

Statistical research: When it comes to the world of IT, machine learning is already making inroads. You will discover that Machine Learning can assist you in sorting through a large amount of complex data in search of large and important patterns. Machine Learning applications in this category will include spam filtering, credit cards, and search engines, among others.

A big data analysis: Many companies have spent time collecting what is known as Big Data, and now they must find a way to sort through and learn from that data in a short amount of time. These businesses can use data to learn more about how their customers spend their money and even to help them make important future decisions. It would take far too long if we had someone go through and do the work manually. But, thanks to Machine Learning, we can complete all of our tasks. Machine Learning has begun to be used in areas such as medicine, election campaigns, and even retail stores to reap some of these benefits.

The financial sector: Many financial institutions have found that Machine Learning can be relied on. Online stock trading, for example, will rely on this type of work, and we will discover that Machine Learning can assist with fraud detection, loan approvals, and other tasks.

To get started with this one and understand how we can get the value we want from Machine Learning, we must ensure that we pair the best algorithms with the right processes and tools. If you use the wrong algorithm to sort through data, you will get a lot of inaccurate information, and the results will not provide you with the assistance that you require. Working with the correct algorithm all of the time will make a significant difference.

The cool thing about this one is that there are a lot of Machine Learning algorithms that we can use to work on your model at this point. Each of these works in a different way than the others, but this ensures that you can handle any problem that arises during the course of your project. Keeping this in mind, you'll notice that some of the different algorithms available include random forests, neural networks, clustering, support vector machines, and others.

As we work on some of the models that we want to create, we will notice that there are a plethora of tools and other processes at our disposal. We need to make sure that we choose the right one so that the algorithm and model that you are working with perform as expected. Machine Learning will provide a variety of tools, including:

1. Integrated management and data quality

2. Automated ensemble evaluation of the model to assist in determining where the best performers will appear.

3. Graphical user interfaces (GUIs) to assist in the creation of the desired models as well as the process flows.

4. Ease of implementation so that you can get results that are reliable and repeatable in a timely manner.

5. Data exploration that is interactive, as well as visualisations that make it easier to see the information

6. An integrated and end-to-end platform to assist with the automation of some of the data-to-decision processes that you would like to follow.

7. A tool for comparing Machine Learning models to assist us in determining the best one to use quickly and efficiently.

Chapter 4: Data Science Algorithms and Models

This guidebook has spent some time going over many of the various aspects of data analysis. We looked at what data analysis is all about, how to work with Python and why it is so useful for data analysis, and even some of the fundamentals of Machine Learning and why it should be a part of our process.

With that in mind, it is now time to move on to some of the other things we can do while working on this process. With the help of the Python programming language, we will investigate some of the best algorithms and models for completing our data analysis. There are numerous algorithms from which to choose, and all of them will be excellent options for completing the task. With that in mind, let's get started and look at some of the best algorithms and models for completing your business data analysis with Python.

Artificial Neural Networks

It's difficult to talk about Machine Learning and data analysis without mentioning neural networks and how these types of coding are supposed to work. Because they work similarly to the human brain, neural networks are an excellent addition to any Machine Learning model. When they get the answer correct, they can learn from it, and some of the synapses that connect everything together will become stronger. The more times this algorithm gets an answer correct, the faster and more efficient it can become at its job.

With neural networks, each of the layers will spend some time at that location to see if there is any pattern. This is frequently done with images or videos, so it will go through each layer of that image to see if it can find a new pattern. If the network identifies one of these patterns, it will initiate the process required to move to the next layer. This is a continuous process in which the neural network goes through many layers until the algorithm has a good idea of what the image is and can make an accurate prediction.

When we reach this point, a few different parts may appear, depending on how the programme is configured. If the algorithm was able to go through the preceding process and sort through all of the different layers, it will make a prediction. If the prediction is correct, the neurons in the system will become stronger than ever. This is because the programme will use artificial intelligence to create the stronger connections and associations required to keep this process going. The more times our neural network returns the correct answer, the more efficient this neural network will become when we use it in the future.

If the programme is properly configured, it will correctly predict that there is a car in the image. The programme can make this prediction based on some of the features of the car that it already knows about, such as the colour, licence plate number, door placement, headlights, and so on.

When using some of the available conventional coding methods, this process can be extremely difficult. You'll discover that the neural network system can make this a very simple system to work with.

You would need to provide the system with an image of the car for the algorithm to work. The neural network would then be able to examine the image. It would begin with the first layer, which would be the car's outside edges. Then it would go through some more layers to help the neural network understand if there are any distinguishing features in the image that indicate it is a car. If the programme is effective at its task, it will improve at detecting even the smallest details about the vehicle, such as its windows and wheel patterns.

This one could have a lot of different layers, but the more layers and details the neural network can find, the more accurately it will be able to predict what kind of car is in front of it. If your neural network correctly identified the car model, it will learn from this lesson. It will remember some of the patterns and characteristics that appeared in the car model and save them for later use. They will be able to make a fairly accurate prediction the next time they encounter the same type of car model.

When working with this algorithm, you will frequently select one and use it when you want to go through a large number of images and find some of the defining features that are contained within them. When working with face recognition software, for example, this type of thing is frequently very useful. With this method, all of the information would not be available ahead of time. Alternatively, you can use this method to teach the computer how to recognise the correct faces.

It is also very effective when it comes to recognising different animals, defining car models, and other tasks.

As you might expect, there are several advantages to working with this type of algorithm. One of these is that we can use this method and not have to worry about the statistics that come with it. Even if you need to work with the algorithm but don't know the statistics or don't have them available, the neural network can be a great option to ensure that any complex relationship is detected.

Bayes' theorem

We can also use an algorithm known as the Nave Bayes algorithm. This is a great algorithm to use whenever you have people who want to see more of the information you're working on and get more involved in the process, but they're unsure how to do so and may not understand the full scope of what you're doing. It is also useful if they want to see these results before the algorithm is completely finished.

As you go through the other algorithms on this page and see what options are available for dealing with the data, you will notice that they frequently handle hundreds of thousands of points of data.

This is why it takes time to train and test the data, and it can be frustrating for those on the outside to discover they must wait before learning anything about the process. When you are just getting started with the whole process, showing information to the people who make the decisions and the key shareholders can be difficult.

Here is where the Nave Bayes algorithm comes into play. It has the potential to make some of your work easier. It is usually not the final algorithm that you use, but it can often give others outside of the process a good idea of what you are doing. It can provide answers to questions, present your work in an easier-to-understand format, and ensure that everyone is on the same page.

Algorithms for clustering

The clustering algorithm is one of the best types of algorithms you can work with. There are several clustering algorithms to choose from, but they will help us ensure that the programme can learn something on its own and handle separating the various data points that we have. These clustering algorithms work best when things are kept simple. It takes some of the data you're working with and creates some clusters that connect. However, before we begin the programme, we can specify the number of clusters to which we want to fit the information.

The number of clusters you choose will also be determined by the type of data you are working with. If all you want to do is separate your customers by gender, you can use just two clusters. If you want to separate the customers based on their age or another factor, you may need to create more clusters. You can select the number of clusters with which to work.

The benefit of clustering algorithms is that they handle the majority of the work of separating and understanding the data for you. This is because the algorithm determines how many data points go into each of the clusters you select, whether you want to work with two or twenty. When you look at one of these clusters, you will notice that with all of the points contained within, it is safe to assume that these data points are similar or share something important. This is why they were placed in the same cluster.

Once we've formed some of these original clusters, we can take each of them and divide them up to get some more sets of clusters, which can sometimes provide us with more insights. We can repeat this a few times to create more division as we progress through the steps. In fact, it is possible to repeat these iterations so many times that the centroids no longer change. This is a sign that the process is nearing completion.

Support Vector Machines (SVMs)

The support vector machine, or SVM, is another option that we must consider. When working with this one, it is critical to take all of the items in our data set and work on plotting them into a single n-dimensional space, rather than scattering them around. N is the number of features that should appear in this algorithm along with the rest of our data. Then we have the option of taking the value of all these features and converting it to the value in your coordinates. From here, we determine the location of the hyperplane, which will show us the differences between our various classes.

When working on this type of algorithm, you may notice that more than one support vector appears. Many of these are easy to dismiss because they are simply the coordinates of individual observations that have been observed. The SVM can then be used as a frontier to separate them into classes. The two support vectors that we must concentrate on are the hyperplane and the line.

To do so, we must first determine the location of the hyperplane. Depending on the type of data we are working with, there may be more than one hyperplane to choose from as we go through this process. There may be an additional challenge because we want to make sure that we choose the option that will help us understand the data rather than one that will lead us astray. The good news is that even if you see more than one option to work with, there are a few steps you can take to make it easier to choose the right one. The steps you can take to make this happen are as follows:

- We'll begin with three hyperplanes, which we'll refer to as 1, 2, and 3. Then we'll spend time determining which hyperplane is correct so that we can classify the star and circle.
- The good news is that there is a fairly simple rule you can follow to help you determine which hyperplane is correct. The hyperplane you want to use will be the one that best separates your classes.
- That one was simple to work with, but in the next one, our hyperplanes 1, 2, and 3 all pass through the classes and segregate them

similarly. For example, all of the lines or hyperplanes will be parallel to one another.

From here, you may find it difficult to determine which hyperplane is the correct one.

For the aforementioned problem, we will need to use what is known as the margin. This is the distance between the hyperplane and the nearest data point in either of the two classes. Then you'll be able to get some numbers that will be useful to you. These numbers may be closer together, but they will reveal which hyperplane is the best.

With the example above, we can see that this is a great tool to use when working with Machine Learning. When we look at some of the available data points, if you notice that there is a pretty good margin that separates some of the points, this is a good place to work with the SVM model. It is effective, and it can also assist us in achieving some of the desired outcomes.

Trees of Decision

Decision trees are another good option for when we want to take a few available options and then compare them to see what the possible outcome of each option is all about. We can even combine a few of these decision trees to create a random forest, which will yield more results and predictions.

The decision tree will be one of the best ways to compare a variety of options and then select the path that is best for your needs. Sometimes we have a plethora of options to choose from, and many of them appear to be excellent ideas.

The decision tree is the best option for businesses that need to choose the best option from a group and know which one is likely to give them the results that they are looking for.

We can use the decision tree to enter the data we have and then see the most likely outcome of making a particular decision. Based on what we see, this prediction can assist us in making sound business decisions. It would be much easier to decide which course of action to take if we had a few different options and could compare the likely outcomes of each one.

K-Closest Neighbors

The next algorithm to consider is the K-Nearest Neighbors algorithm, abbreviated as KNN. When we use this algorithm, the goal is to search through all of our data for the k most similar example of any instance that we want to work with. Once we have finished this process, the algorithm can proceed to the next step, which is to go through all of the information you have and provide you with a summary. The algorithm will then take those results and provide you with some of the predictions you require to make sound business decisions.

You will notice that as you use this learning algorithm, the learning you are working with becomes more competitive. This works in your favour because there will be a lot of competition between the different elements or parts of the models so that you can get the best solution or prediction based on the data you have.

When it comes to working with this algorithm, there are several advantages that we can reap. For example, it is excellent for cutting through the noise that sometimes appears in our data. This noise, depending on the set of data that you use, can be quite loud, and reducing it can help make a significant difference in the insights that you can see.

And if you're trying to handle and then sort through some of the larger amounts of data that some businesses have all at once, this is a great algorithm to use. Unlike some of the others, which must limit the set of data by a bit, the KNN algorithm can handle all of your data, no matter how large it is.

Keep in mind that the computational costs of this method are sometimes higher, but in some cases, this isn't such a big deal to work with.

There are a few steps that you can take to make the K-Nearest Neighbors algorithm work the way you want it to.

Working with this algorithm can help us get a lot done when it comes to putting parts together and determining where all of our data is supposed to lie. If you follow the steps outlined above, you will be able to complete this model for yourself and see some fantastic results when it comes time to make predictions and good business decisions.

The Markov Chain Algorithm

The Markov algorithm is another type of unsupervised Machine Learning algorithm that you can use. This algorithm will take the data that you choose to input into it and then translate it to help work in another coding language if you choose.

The nice thing about this algorithm is that you can choose which rules to use with it ahead of time so that it works the way you want it to. Many Machine

Learning programmers appreciate this algorithm, as well as the ability to set up their own rules ahead of time, because it allows you to take a string of data and ensure that it is as useful as possible as you learn on the job and figure out the parameters of how the data will behave.

Another advantage of this Markov algorithm is that you can use it in a variety of ways rather than being limited to just one. One thing to keep in mind is that this algorithm works well with things like DNA. For example, you could take someone's DNA sequence and use this algorithm to convert the information contained within that sequence into numerical values.

This can often make it easier for programmers, doctors, scientists, and others to understand what information is available and make better predictions for the future. When working with programmers and computers, you will discover that numerical data is much easier to sort through than other methods of looking through DNA.

A good reason to use the Markov algorithm is that it is excellent at learning problems when you know the input you want to use but are unsure about the parameters. This algorithm will be able to discover insights hidden within the data. In some cases, these insights are hidden, making it difficult for the other algorithms we've discussed to find them. There are still some drawbacks to using the Markov algorithm.

This one can be difficult to work with at times because you must manually go through and create a new rule every time you want to add a new programming language. If you only intend to use one type of programming language on your project, this will not be a problem. However, your programme will frequently need to work with multiple languages, and going in and creating new rules a number of times can become tedious.

Chapter 5: Regression Analysis (Linear and Logistic Regression)

Several industries around the world are grappling with the best way to gather the right data or information that will eventually allow them to solve their recurring prediction problems. Several banks have suffered losses, particularly in their credit division, because they were unable to accurately predict the trustworthiness of the defaulters.

Many people have died in the health care sector as a result of poor planning and risk management, which result from a lack of modelling to tool for more straightforward prediction. We also have other sectors, such as weather forecasting, where farmers were not informed of the occurrence of rain, resulting in increased losses. Another issue was the payment of mortgages by homeowners. As a result of all of this, everyone in the universe went on a rampage in search of the best possible way to handle the prediction roles of the organizations. All of this culminated in what is now known as regression analysis.

As a result, regression analysis refers to statistical processes for predicting outcomes based on variables. It aids in identifying the variables' relationships. This study includes both independent and dependent variables. In other words, regression analysis helps understand the effect of one independent variable on the dependent variable when the other independent variables are held constant. Most of the time, regression analysis will make every effort to predict the conditional expectation, particularly of the dependent variable.

Regression analysis is used in a variety of fields, including weather forecasting and prediction. In this case, it aids in predicting the outcome of the rain over a specific time period. It is also useful in other fields, such as medicine, for predicting the likelihood of diseases.

Regression analysis includes the following techniques: linear regression, logistic regression, polynomial regression, stepwise regression, ridge, lasso, and elastic net regression. Overall, this chapter will only cover the most commonly used regression analysis techniques, such as linear regression and logistic regression. It is worth noting that ElasticNet regression is a hybrid of the Lasso and Ridge regression methods.

Regression Linear

Linear regression is a statistical method for modelling a relationship between several variables in a given set of independent variables. In this chapter, you'll learn more about dependent variables like response and independent variables like simplicity. To be able to provide extensive search results and a clear understanding of linear regression in Python, you must be keen on a fundamental level. We'll start with the most basic version of the subject. What, for example, is a simple linear regression?

By definition, simple linear regression is a significant approach for predicting a significant response using a single feature. As a result, it is assumed that the two main variables in this case are directly related. That is why it is critical to determine the linear function because it frequently accurately predicts the main response value of the equation. There are various regression models that are used to demonstrate and predict the main relationship between two different variables and factors. As a result, it's critical to remember that the main factor being predicted is referred to as the dependent variable. However, the factors used to predict the main value of the dependent variable are referred to as the independent variable. With that said, it's also important to note that good data doesn't always tell the whole storey. As a result, regression analysis is frequently used in research and the determination of variable correlations. Correlation, on the other hand, is not the same as the subject of causation. As a result, a line found in a simple linear regression that is appropriately fitting into the data points may not indicate a definitive element in a major cause and effect relationship.

In the case of linear regression, each observation has two values. As a result, one of the values is specific to the dependent variable. The other is without a doubt for the independent variable.

Python Linear Regression

When we talk about simple linear regression analysis, we're looking at some of the most basic types of regression analysis that can be used on multiple independent variables as well as one independent variable.

As a result, in such a model, a straight line is frequently used to approximate the main relationship between an independent and a dependent variable. When two major independent variables are used in regression analysis, multiple regression analysis occurs. As a result, the model will not be a slightly simplified linear one. This model (y= 0 + 1 + E.) is typically used to represent a simple linear regression.

Two major factors are involved herein by applying the relevant mathematical convention. They include the main designations, x and y. In addition, the equation frequently describes how y correlates with x. This is referred to as the regression model. Aside from that, the linear regression model includes an error term, which is commonly denoted by E. It is also known as the Greek letter epsilon.

Typically, this error term is used to account for the variability in y. This element, however, cannot be explained in terms of the linear relationship found between x and y. It's also worth noting that the parameters represent the main population being studied. Some of these parameters are representative of the main population being studied. A regression line, in most cases, can easily show how a unique positive linear relationship, no relationship, and a negative relationship.

That being said, if the graphed line appears to be in a simple linear regression that is flat in any way, no relationship between the two variables will be found. If, on the other hand, the regression line slopes upwards, with the lower end of the line located at y on the graph, then there is a positive linear relationship within the graph. However, if the regression line has a tendency to slope downward where the upper end of y intersects the graph's axis. When the parameters are well identified and known, the equation of simple linear regression can use the computed meaning of the value of y.

However, in practise, various parameter values are unknown.

As a result, they must be estimated using data sampling from the actual population. As a result, sample statistics are frequently used to estimate the parameters of these populations. b0 + b1 can be used to represent these statistics.

It is obvious that we live in a world that necessitates the use of massive amounts of data, powerful computers, and artificial intelligence.

While this is only the beginning, there is a growing use of Data Science in a variety of industries around the world. Machine learning is also driving image recognition, autonomous vehicle development, and decision-making in the finance and energy industries.

As a result, linear regression in Python remains a fundamental statistical and Machine Learning technique. As a result, for those interested in statistics or scientific computing, this is likely to be a requirement in the course work. It is not only advisable to engage in the learning process, but also to progress to various complex methods added to the studies.

It is critical to understand the various types of linear regression.

One of them is multiple linear regressions, which are a special case of linear regression with two or more independent variables. As a result, when there are two independent variables, the probable regression function will represent a major regression plane in a three-dimensional space. As a result, the value that will determine different weights appears to be the goal of the regression. This also happens to be the closest match to the actual response. In a different scenario, the case where two independent variables exceed each other is frequently similar.

However, it is also more general. In a similar vein, you could consider polynomial regression to be a significant generalised issue of linear regression in Python. Having said that, you can easily assume the polynomial dependence found between the output and inputs.

In that case, your regression function may also be f, which may contain other non-linear terms.

In most cases, linear regression is the first Machine Learning algorithm that data scientists encounter in their work. It's a critical model that everyone in the industry should understand. This is due to the fact that it aids in the establishment of a solid foundation for various Machine Learning algorithms.

For starters, it can be used to forecast sales by analysing sales data from the first few months. It may also be used to gain valuable insight into consumer behaviour.

Logistic Regression

Logistic regression is made up of many different components, including a logistic model, a logistic function, a statistics model, and much more. As a result, many organisations use logistic regression in their day-to-day operations, which are primarily comprised of data predictions and analysis. This regression analysis is always possible, especially when the dependent variable is binary. That's a dichotomy.

Logistic regression, like other types of regression analyses, is completely applicable in any prediction analysis. In this case, its primary function is to describe data. Furthermore, logistic regression can be used to explain or illustrate the type of relationship that exists between the binary variable, which is the dependent variable, and the other variables, which are independent variables. This regression may appear difficult to interpret, but with the assistance of specific tools such as Intellectus Statistics, you can easily conduct your data analysis.

With the help of the logistic model, logistic regression knowledge can be easily applied in statistics. In this case, the primary function of the logistic model is to use probability to arrive at the correct results of certain predictions or classes. Probability, for example, works best when you only need to predict the outcome of existing events. These events include: being healthy or sick, winning or losing, being alive or dead, or even being in places where you are analysing whether someone passes or fails a test. Nonetheless, you will be able to fine-tune your result in this model primarily through probability. In the case of an image, you will be able to extend your model to include multiple classes. You'll be able to tell whether the image in your analysis is a lion or a cat, for example. In this case, the individual variables within the image will have probabilities ranging from 0 to 1. However, the total here should equal one.

As a result, logistic regression refers to a fundamental statistical model that makes greater use of the available logistic function, regardless of the complexity of additional extensions that may exist. Logistic regression is an integral part of regression analysis, and it is frequently used in various analyses where logistic model parameters are estimated. Remember that the logistic model is a type of binary regression. As a result, a binary regression is made up of a binary logistic model. This model is made up of a dependent variable with two possible event values. These values can be represented in a variety of ways, including pass/fail, alive/dead, good/bad, and many others. It is important to note that the indicator variable actually denotes these possible values, which are always labelled 0 and 1. Within this logistic model, the odds logarithm, or log-odds, represents a linear combination for values of 1. This combination contains one or more variables that are completely independent of one another. In this case, they are referred to as predictors.

Furthermore, in logistic regression analysis, independent variables may form a binary variable or a continuous variable. In the case of a binary variable, there must be two classes or events, which must be coded by the indicator variables. Continuous variables, on the other hand, represent real value. As previously stated, the corresponding probability of these values varies between 0 and 1 in the logistic regression analysis. In this analysis, these log-odds, or algorithms of odds, will be converted into probability by a logistic function. Log odds are measured in logit, which is also derived from its name (logistic unit). Again, a probit model with a different sigmoid function can be used to convert the log odds into a probability for easy analysis. It is worth noting that the probit model is an example of an analogous model that includes the sigmoid function.

Overall, the logistic model is the most preferred in this conversion due to its distinguishing attributes or characteristics. The logistic model's ability to increase the multiplicatively scales of each of the independent variables is one such feature. As a result, it generates a result with parameters assigned to each independent variable at a constant rate. However, if the odd ratio is part of a variable with a binary dependent, this will generalise it.

It is also worth noting that there are extensions for dependent variables, particularly in some regressions such as binary logistic. This extension, however, is only applicable when two or more levels are used. These two extensions include multinomial logistic regression, which works best with categorical outputs, particularly those with multiple values (two or more). The ordinal logistic regression is the next type of logistic regression extension, which deals with a large collection of multiple categories. The ordinal logistic model, which deals with proportional odds, is a good example here. However, because it is not a classifier, this system only performs modelling and does not perform any classifications based on statistics. As a result, it will only transform the probability input into an output. Following that, we'll look at how logistic regression can be used in real-world scenarios.

Logistic Regression Applications

Logistic regression is used by meteorologists in metrological and other forecasting stations. The algorithm in this case is used to forecast the likelihood of rain. This information is critical because it aids in a variety of industries, including agriculture and transportation. Planting time can be efficiently planned for, and the proper arrangement can be put in place.

This analysis is also used in some risk management systems, such as credit control. In this case, the analysis will predict whether or not the account holder is a payment defaulter.

Still, using the previous records, the regression analysis will predict the exact amount that someone can be given. This also allows many organisations to function because they have complete control over risk management. Before any credit is applied to any account, it will be thoroughly reviewed. Logistic regression is also used in the political sector, particularly during elections. It gives the probability of winning and losing for each candidate based on their strengths and resources used. Again, this regression analysis will be able to predict the number of people who will not vote, as well as who will vote in the end and for which candidate.

Some factors that influence the prediction outcome include the candidate's age, gender, income of both the candidate and the voters, state of residence of both, and total number of votes cast in the previous elections.

Logistic regression is also used in a variety of medical fields. It's used in epidemiology. In this case, the analysis is used to identify all of the risk factors that may lead to disease. Precautions and other preventive measures may be implemented as a result.

Its knowledge can be applied to the Trauma and Injury Severity Score (TRISS), which predicts mortality, particularly in injured patients. We have several medical scales that have been developed to assess the severity of patients all over the world.

All of these medical scales were created or managed with the help of logistic regression. In most cases, particularly in the health sector, this knowledge can be used to predict the risk of contracting some dangerous diseases. Diseases such as coronary heart disease, diabetes, and other health-related complications, for example, are easily controlled. These forecasts are based on the individual patient's observable characteristics on a daily basis. Body mass index, sex, age, and even different blood test results are examples of traits or characteristics. This will eventually aid in proper medical planning and risk management.

This knowledge can also be applied in the engineering field.

It is used in this context to predict the failure probability of a specific system, a new product, or even any type of process. In the field of marketing, logistic regression analysis aids in determining buyers' purchasing power and proclivity to purchase, and this knowledge can also be used to halt various company subscriptions. The method is also used in economics. In this case, knowledge is used to forecast the outcome of working in the public sector. This method is also used in issues involving the likelihood of homeowners failing to make mortgage payments. Natural language processing employs conditional random fields, which are a logistic regression extension, particularly for sequential data.

Linear Regression vs. Logistic Regression

You might be wondering what the main difference is between these two regression examples. In terms of outcome, linear regression is responsible for continuous prediction, whereas logistic regression has a discrete outcome. A model that predicts the price of a car will take into account various factors such as colour, year of manufacture, and so on. As a result, this value will always be different, indicating a continuous result. A discrete outcome, on the other hand, is always one thing. That is, in the event of illness, you can either be sick or not be sick.

Advantages of logistic regression - It is very effective and efficient - You can get an outcome without requiring large computational resources - You can easily interpret it - There are no input features required for the scaling process - There is no tuning required - You can easily regularise logistic regression

How Does Machine Learning Differ From AI?

Before we move on, we need to spend some time working on and understanding the difference between Artificial Intelligence and Machine Learning. When we look at the field of Data

Science, machine learning will perform a variety of tasks, and it also falls under the category of artificial intelligence.

However, we must recognise that Data Science is a broad term with numerous concepts that will fall under it. Machine Learning is one of these concepts that fall under the umbrella of Data Science, but we will also see terms like big data, data mining, and artificial intelligence. Data Science is a newer field that is expanding as people discover new applications for computers and use them more frequently.

When it comes to Data Science, you can also focus on the field of statistics, which is frequently combined with Machine Learning. Even at the highest levels, you can work with a focus on classical statistics to ensure that the data set remains consistent throughout. Of course, the various methods that you use to accomplish this will vary depending on the type of data that is entered and how complex the information that you are using becomes.

This raises the question of the distinctions that exist between Machine Learning and Artificial Intelligence and why they are not the same thing. There are many similarities between these two options, but the major differences are what distinguishes them, and any programmer who wants to work with Machine Learning must understand some of the differences that emerge.

Let's spend some time here exploring the various components of artificial intelligence and machine learning to see how they are similar and how they differ.

What exactly is Artificial Intelligence (AI)?

The first topic we'll look at is artificial intelligence, abbreviated as AI. In the 1950s, a computer scientist named John McCarthy coined the term. AI was initially described as a method for manufactured devices to learn how to mimic the capabilities of humans in terms of mental tasks.

However, the term has evolved slightly in modern times, but the basic concept remains the same. When you implement AI, you are allowing machines, such as computers, to operate and think in the same way that the human brain does. This is a benefit because it means that these AI devices will be more efficient than the human brain at completing certain tasks.

At first glance, it may appear that AI and Machine Learning are the same thing, but they are not. Some people who don't understand how these two terms work may believe they are the same, but how you use them in programming will make a big difference.

What distinguishes Machine Learning?

Now that we understand what artificial intelligence is all about, let's look at Machine Learning and how it is similar to and different from artificial intelligence. When we look at Machine Learning, we will notice that it is a bit newer than some of the other options that come with Data Science, having only been around for about 20 years. Despite the fact that it has been around for a few decades, it has only been in the last few years that our technology and machines have been able to catch up to this and Machine Learning is being used more.

Machine learning is distinct in that it is a subset of Data Science that can focus solely on having the programme learn from the input as well as the data that the user provides. This is useful because the algorithm will be able to use that data to make some accurate predictions. Let's take a look at an example of how to use a search engine. To make this work, simply enter a term into a search query, and the search engine will be able to look through the information to see what matches up with that and return some results.

The first few times you run these search queries, the results are likely to include something of interest, but you may need to scroll down the page a bit to find the information that you seek. However, as you continue to do so, the computer will take that information and learn from it in order to provide you with better choices in the future. You might click on the sixth result the first time, but after a while, you might click on the first or second result because the computer has learned what you value.

This is not something that your computer can do on its own with traditional programming. Everyone searches differently, and there are millions of pages to sort through. Furthermore, each person conducting an online search will have preferences for what they want to see. When you try to do this kind of task with traditional programming, you will run into problems because there are simply too many variables. Machine learning, on the other hand, has the potential to make it happen.

Of course, this is only one example of how Machine Learning can be used. In fact, Machine Learning can assist you in solving some of the more complex problems you want the computer to solve. Sometimes the human brain can solve these problems, but more often than not, Machine Learning is more efficient and faster than the human brain.

Of course, you could have someone manually go through and do this for you, but you can imagine that this would take a long time and be a massive undertaking. There is too much information, they may not know where to begin sorting through it, the information can confuse them, and by the time they get through it all, too much time has passed and the information, as well as the predictions that come from it, are no longer relevant to the company at all.

Because it can keep up, machine learning changes the game. The algorithms that can be used with it can handle all of the work while providing you with the results you require in almost real-time. This is one of the main reasons why businesses believe it is one of the best options to help them make good and sound decisions, predict the future, and is a welcome addition to their business model.

Chapter 6: Interaction with Databases

Data management is not a scientific discipline in and of itself. However, it is increasingly permeating basic scientific work. The increasing volume and complexity of data have long outpaced the ability of simple spreadsheets to manage it.

Currently, it is very common to need to store quantitative, qualitative data, and media in various formats (images, videos, sounds) in an integrated platform from which they can be easily accessed for analysis, visualisation, or simply consultation.

At its most sophisticated levels of sophistication, the Python language has simple solutions to this need. Following the included batteries, the Python standard library introduces us to the Pickle and cPickle modules, as well as, beginning with Version 2.5, the SQLite3 relational database.

Pickling Module

The pickle module and its faster cousin, cPickle, implement algorithms that allow you to save Python-implemented objects to a file.

An example of how to use the pickle module

pickle import

def say hi (self): print " hi " a= hi() f= open ('pic test','w')

pickle.dump(a, f) f.close() f= open ('pic test','r') f= open ('pic test','r')

(f) b.say hi b=pickle.load ()

hi

As demonstrated by the use of the pickle module, we can store objects in a file and retrieve them without difficulty for later use. However, in Example 8.1, an important feature of this module is missing. When an object is stored with the pickle module, neither the class code nor its data are included; only the instance data is included.

def say hi (self, name=' alex'): print'hi percent s!' percent

name

open ('pictest','r') f

b=pickle.load b=pickle.load b=pickle.load (f)

b.say hi()

hello, Alex!

As shown above, we can modify the class and the stored instance will recognise the new code as it is restored from the file. This feature ensures that pickles do not become obsolete when the code on which they are based is updated (though this is only true for changes that do not remove attributes already included in the pickles).

The pickle module is designed not just for data storage, but also for complex computational objects that may contain data. Despite its versatility, this is due to the fact that it is only readable by the pickle module in a Python programme.

SQLite3 is a database module.

With Python 2.5, this module becomes a standard part of the Python library. As a result, it is an excellent choice for users who require the functionality of a SQL1-compliant relational database.

SQLite evolved from a C library with an extremely lightweight database and no client-server concept. The database in SQLite is a file that is managed by the SQLite library.

Importing the SQLite3 module is required to use SQLite in a Python programme.

sqlite3 import

The next step is to create a connection object, which will allow us to execute SQL commands.

sqlite 3.connect ('/tmp/ example') c= sqlite 3.connect ('/tmp/ example')

We now have an empty database with the example file in the / tmp directory. SQLite can also be used to create RAM databases. Simply replace the file name with the string: memory to accomplish this. We must first create a table in order to insert data into this database.

c.execute ("'generate table specimens (name text, true height, true weight)"')

sqlite 3.Cursor object located at 0 x83fed10 >

SQL commands are sent as strings via the Connection object's execute method. The create table command creates a table; it must be followed by the table name and a list of typed variables (in parentheses) that correspond to the variables in this table. This command only creates the table structure. Each variable specified will correspond to one column of the table. Each entry after that will form a table row.

c.execute ("'insert values (' tom', 1 2.5, 2.3) into specimens"'

Another useful SQL command for inserting records into a table is insert.

Although SQL commands are sent as strings over the connection, using Python's string formatting methods ('... values (percent s, percent s)' percent (1,2)) is not recommended for security reasons. Instead, carry out the following actions:

t= ('tom,')

c.execute ('from specimens where name=?', t)

c.retrieve all ()

[('tom', 1 2.5, 2.2 9 9 9 9 9 9 9 9 9 9 9 9 9 9 9 9 9 9 9 9 9 9 9 9 9 9 9 9 9 9 9 9 9 9 9 9 9 9 9 9 9 9 9 9 9 9 9 9 9 9 9 9 9 9 9 9 9 9 9 9

In the preceding example, we use the fetchall method to retrieve the operation's result. If we only wanted one record, we would use fetchone.

Here's how to insert multiple records from existing data structures. In this case, it is simply a matter of repeating the previous example's operation with a sequence of tubes representing the sequence of records to be inserted.

T = (('jerry, 5.1, 0.2), ('butch, 4 2.4, 1 0.3)) for I in t:

c.execute (' insert into specimens value s (?,?,?)', I The cursor object can also be used to iterate over the results of a query.

c.execute ('select from specimens by weight') in c for reg:

print reg ('jerry', 5.1, 0.2) ('tom', 1 2.5, 2.2 9 9 9 9 9 9 9 9 9 9 9 9 9 9 9 9 9 9 9 9 9 9 9 9 9 9 9 9 9 9 9 9 9 9 9 9 9 9 9 9 9 9 9 9 9 9 9 9 9 9 9 9 9 9 9 9 9 9 9 9 9 9 9 9 9 9 9 9 9 9 9 9 9 9 9 9 9 9 9 9 9 9 9 9 9 9 9 9 9 9 9 9

The SQLite module is extremely versatile and useful, but it does necessitate that the user understand the fundamentals of the SQL language. The solution that follows attempts to solve this problem in a more Pythonic manner.

SQLObject is a package.

The SQLObject2 package extends the previous solutions in two ways: it provides an object-oriented interface to relational databases and allows us to interact with multiple databases without changing our code.

We will continue to use SQLite as an example of sqlobject due to its practicality.

Making a Virtual Spider

In this example, we will be able to create a digital spider that will collect information from the web (Wikipedia3) and store it in a SQLite bank using sqlobject.

We'll need some tools that go beyond the database for this example. Let's look at the standard Python library's ability to interact with the internet, and then use an external package to decode the pages we get.

BeautifulSoup4package is a website killer. One of the most common issues with HTML pages is that many of them have minor design flaws that our browsers ignore but can impede further examination.

As a result, BeautifulSoup adds value by handling faulty pages and returning a data structure with methods for quick and easy extraction of the desired information. Furthermore, if the page was created with a different encoding, BeautifulSoup automatically returns all Unicode content without user intervention.

We will use the sys, os, urllib, urllib2, and re modules from the standard library. As the example progresses, the utility of each character becomes clear.

The initial step is to define the database. SQLObject provides us with the option of using MySQL, PostgreSQL, SQLite, Firebird, MAXDB, Sybase, MSSQL, or ADODBAPI. However, as previously stated, we will limit ourselves to using the SQLite database.

Defining the Database

If os.path.exists (at the dir), johnsmith= os.path.expanduser (' /. johnsmith'):

mkdir os (at the dir)

sqlhub.process Connection = connectionForURI (' sqlite:/' + johnsmithr + '/knowdb')

When we specify the database, we create the directory (os.mkdir) where the database will reside (if necessary), and we connect to the database natively. To see if the directory exists, we use os.path.exists.

We use os.path.expanduser to replace / home/user on the Unix console because we want the directory in the user's folder and have no way of knowing what this directory is.

We see the command that creates the connection that will be used by all objects created in this module on line 11 of Specifying the database.

Following that, we define our database table as a class, with the table columns as its attributes.

Defining the database concepttable.

Idea for a class (SQLObject): UnicodeCol name= () IntCol nlinks ()

Pickle Collecting () StringCol = address

The SQLObject class is inherited by the class that represents our table. Each attribute (table column) in this class must be assigned an object that specifies the type of data to be stored. There are four distinct types in this example, but there are many more. UnicodeCol represents Unicode-encoded texts, which can contain characters from any language. Integer numbers are represented by IntCol. PickleCol is a fascinating type because it can store any type of Python object.

The most intriguing aspect of this type of column is that it does not necessitate the use of the pickle module to store or read this type of variable. Variables are converted/converted automatically based on the operation. Finally, StringCol is a simplified version of UnicodeCol that accepts only ASCII character strings. It is common in SQL to have terms that specify different types based on the length of the text you want to store in a variable. There is no limit to the size of text that can be stored in StringCol or UnicodeCol in sqlobject.

Our spider's functionality has been divided into two classes: Crawler, which is the creeper itself, and UrlFac, which builds URLs from the word you want in Wikipedia.

The urllib2 module retrieves each page. The urllib module's urlencode function makes it simple to add data to our request so that it does not appear to be from a digital spider. Without this guise, Wikipedia rejects the link.

The pages are then parsed by the VerResp method, which allows BeautifulSoup to do its work. Using the SoupStrainer function, we can find the rest of the document that isn't of interest to us by analysing only the links (tags 'a') whose destination is a URL that starts with the string/wiki/. This is how all Wikipedia articles begin.

As a result, we avoid chasing external links. Only the URLs, i.e. what comes after "href =", are extracted from the soup.

Chapter 7: Data Mining Techniques in Data Science

The fundamentals of math and statistics aid a data scientist in the development, analysis, and creation of complex analytics. Data scientists must interact with the business side in order to gain accurate insights from the data. When it comes to analysing data to help the business, business acumen is required. The outcomes must also meet the expectations of the businesses. As a result, the ability to verbally and visually communicate advanced results and observations to the business and assist them in understanding is essential. Data Mining is a Data Science strategy that describes the process of structuring raw data in such a way that mathematical and computational algorithms can recognise patterns in the data. Let's take a look at five major data mining techniques that every data scientist should be familiar with.

Technique of Mapreduce

Data Mining applications constantly manage massive amounts of data.

To deal with such applications, you must choose a new software stack.

Stack software stores its file system, which is known as a distributed file system. This file system is used to retrieve parallelism from a computing cluster or clusters of computing clusters. This distributed file system replicates data to ensure data security in the event of a media failure. Aside from this stack file system, a higher-level programming system known as Mapreduce has been developed to help with the process. Mapreduce is a type of computation that is used in a variety of systems, including Hadoop and Google.

Mapreduce is a data mining technique for dealing with large-scale computations. It is simple to implement, as you only need to type three functions: Map and Reduce. The system will control parallel execution and task collaboration automatically.

Distance Metrics

The primary limitation of data mining is the inability to track similar data/items. Consider the situation in which you must track duplicate websites or web content while browsing various websites. Another example is finding similar images in a large database.

You can use the Distance Measure technique to solve such problems. Distance Measure aids in the search for nearest neighbours in a three-dimensional space. It is critical to define what is meant by similarity. Jaccard One such example is similarity. The following methods are used to identify similarity and define the Distance Measure Technique:

Shingling \Min-Hashing Locality Hashing That Is Sensitive

A Locality-Sensitive K-Shingle Hashing

Link Examining

When you can scan the spam vulnerabilities, you can perform link analysis. Previously, most traditional search engines failed to scan for spam vulnerabilities. However, as technology advanced, Google was able to implement some techniques to address this issue.

Pagerank

Pagerank techniques employ the simulation method. It scans every page you visit for spam vulnerabilities. This entire process is iterative, which means that pages with a higher number of visitors are ranked higher than pages with no visitors.

The Information

Some specific phrases used in a page to link with external pages determine the content on each page. Spammers can easily modify the internal pages where they are administrators, but it is more difficult for them to modify the external pages. A function assigns a real number to each page. The page with a higher rank becomes more important than the page without a significant page rank. There are no algorithms in place to assign ranks to pages. They do, however, have a transition matrix-based ranking for highly confidential or connected Web Graphics. This principle is used to determine a page's rank.

Streaming Data

It can be difficult to predict datasets in advance; additionally, data appears in the form of a stream and is processed before disappearing. Data arrives at such a rapid rate that it is difficult to store it in active storage. Data streaming enters the picture here. An infinite number of streams can be stored in a system using the dataStream management system. Every data stream generates elements at its own pace. In a given stream cycle, elements move at the same rate and at the same time. These streams are saved in the store. This makes it more difficult to respond to queries that have already been saved in the archive. However, such circumstances are handled by specific retrieval methods. There is a working store as well as an active store that stores summaries in order to respond to specific queries. There are some data Streaming issues. viz.

Data Sampling in a Stream

You will select attributes to generate some stream samples. You must rotate the hashing key of the incoming stream element to determine whether all of the sample elements belong to the same key sample.

Stream Filtering

There is a separate process for selecting specific tuples to fit a specific criterion, in which accepted tuples are carried forward while others are terminated and eliminated. Bloon Filtering is a modern technique that will allow you to filter out foreign elements. Later, the selected elements are hashed and collected into buckets to form bits. Bits operate in binary mode, i.e., 0 and 1. These bits are set to 1. Following that, the elements are ready to be tested.

Count Individual Elements in a Stream

If you need to count the unique elements in a universal set, you may have to count each element starting from the first step.

Flajolet-Martin is a method for hashing elements to integers, also known as binary numbers. The use of hash functions and their integration may result in a reliable estimate.

Analysis of Frequent Item – Set

We will examine the market-basket model and its relationship in Frequent Item Set Analysis. Every basket contains a specific set of items, whereas the market will have data. The total number of items is always greater than the total number of basket items. This implies that the number of items in the basket can be accommodated in the memory. Baskets are the original and genuine files in the distributed system as a whole. Each basket contains a specific type of item. To summarise the market-basket technique, the characterization of data is dependent on this technique to discover common itemsets. These groups of items are responsible for revealing the majority of the baskets. There are numerous use cases for this technique available on the Internet. This technique has previously been used in large malls, supermarkets, and chain stores. As an example, such stores keep track of each basket that a customer brings to the checkout counter.

Items represent the store's products, whereas baskets are a collection of items found in a single basket.

Chapter 8: Decision Trees

Decision trees are similar to support vector machines in that they are a type of supervised machine learning algorithm that can solve both regression and classification problems. They are effective when dealing with large amounts of data.

You must go beyond the fundamentals in order to process large and complex datasets. Furthermore, decision trees are used in the construction of random forests, which are widely regarded as the most powerful learning algorithm. Because of their popularity and efficiency, we will exclusively focus on decision trees in this chapter.

A Quick Overview of Decision Trees

Decision trees are essentially a tool that supports a decision that will influence all subsequent decisions. This means that everything from expected outcomes to consequences and resource utilisation will be influenced in some way. Take note that decision trees are typically represented in a graph, which can be thought of as a type of chart in which the training tests appear as nodes. For example, the node could be a coin toss with two possible outcomes. Furthermore, branches sprout to represent the results individually, and they have leaves that serve as class labels. You can see why this algorithm is referred to as a decision tree now. The structure is reminiscent of a tree. Random forests are, as you might expect, exactly what they sound like.

They are collections of decision trees, but that's all there is to it.

Decision trees are one of the most powerful supervised learning methods, particularly for beginners. Unlike more complex algorithms, they are relatively simple to implement and have a lot to offer. Any common Data Science task can be performed by a decision tree, and the results obtained at the end of the training process are highly accurate. With that in mind, let's look at a few more benefits and drawbacks to gain a better understanding of their use and implementation.

Let's start with the good news:

Decision trees are simple in design and thus simple to implement, even if you have no formal education in Data Science or machine learning. This algorithm's concept can be summarised with a formula that follows a common type of programming statement: If this, then that, else that. Furthermore, the results will be very simple to interpret, thanks to the graphic representation.

The second benefit is that a decision tree is one of the most efficient methods for exploring and determining the most important variables, as well as discovering the relationship between them. You can also easily create new features to improve measurements and predictions. Don't forget that data exploration is one of the most important stages of working with data, especially when there are a lot of variables to consider. To avoid a time-consuming process, you must be able to detect the most valuable ones, and decision trees excel at this.

Another advantage of implementing decision trees is that they are excellent at removing outliers from your data. Remember that outliers are noise that lowers the accuracy of your predictions. Furthermore, noise has little effect on decision trees. Outliers have such a small impact on this algorithm in many cases that you can choose to ignore them if you don't need to maximise the accuracy scores.

Finally, decision trees are capable of working with both numerical and categorical variables. Keep in mind that some of the algorithms we've already discussed can only be used with one type of data or the other. Decision trees, on the other hand, have been shown to be versatile and capable of handling a much broader range of tasks.

As you can see, decision trees are extremely powerful, versatile, and simple to implement, so why would we use anything else? As is customary, nothing is perfect, so let's look at the drawbacks of using this type of algorithm:

Overfitting is a major issue that arises during the implementation of a decision tree. Take note that this algorithm has a tendency to generate very complicated decision trees that, due to their complexity, will have difficulty generalising data. This is referred to as overfitting, and it occurs when implementing other learning algorithms as well, though not to the same extent. Fortunately, this does not preclude you from employing decision trees.

To reduce the impact of overfitting, all you need to do is invest some time in implementing certain parameter limitations.

Continuous variables can cause problems for decision trees. When dealing with continuous numerical variables, decision trees lose some information. This issue arises when the variables are classified. A continuous variable is a value that is set to be within a range of numbers if you are unfamiliar with them. If people between the ages of 18 and 26 are considered to be of student age, then this numerical range becomes a continuous variable because it can hold any value between the declared minimum and maximum.

While some disadvantages may necessitate additional work in the implementation of decision trees, the benefits far outweigh them.

Trees for Classification and Regression

We previously discussed how decision trees are used for both regression and classification tasks. However, this does not imply that you use the same decision trees in both cases. Classification and regression trees must be separated from decision trees.

They deal with different problems, but they are related in some ways because they are both types of decision trees.

Keep in mind that classification decision trees are used when the dependent variable is categorical. A regression tree, on the other hand, is only used when the dependent variable is continuous. Furthermore, in the case of a classification tree, the training data result is the mode of the total relevant observations. This means that any observations that we cannot define will be predicted based on this value, which represents the most frequently identified observation.

Regression trees, on the other hand, operate in a slightly different manner. The value obtained during the training stage is not the mode value, but rather the mean of all observations. As a result, the unidentified observations are declared with the mean value derived from the known observations.

Both types of decision trees go through a binary split from top to bottom. This means that observations in one area will generate two branches, which will then be divided within the predictor space.

This is also referred to as a greedy approach because the learning algorithm seeks the most relevant variable in the split while ignoring future splits that could lead to the development of a more powerful and accurate decision tree.

As you can see, the two have some differences as well as similarities. What you should take away from all of this is that the splitting has the greatest impact on the decision tree implementation's accuracy scores. Regardless of the type of tree, decision tree nodes are divided into subnodes. This tree split is carried out to produce a more uniform set of nodes.

Now that you've grasped the fundamentals of decision trees, let's delve a little deeper into the issue of overfitting.

The Overfitting Issue

Overfitting is one of the most common issues when working with decision trees, and it can have a significant impact on the results. If no constraints are imposed, decision trees can achieve a 100 percent accuracy score for the training set. The major disadvantage here is that overfitting occurs when the algorithm attempts to eliminate training errors while actually increasing testing errors. Regardless of the score, this imbalance leads to poor prediction accuracy in the end result. What causes this to happen?

In this case, the decision trees grow a lot of branches, which causes overfitting. To solve this, set limits on how much the decision tree can grow and how many branches it can produce.

Furthermore, you can prune the tree to keep it under control, just as you would with a real tree to ensure it produces a plentiful supply of fruit.

To limit the size of the decision tree, you must define new parameters during the tree's definition. Let's look at these parameters:

1. split minimal samples: The first thing you can do is change this parameter to specify how many observations a node needs to be able to split. You can declare anything with a sample count ranging from one to a maximum of ten. Just keep in mind that increasing the value will prevent the training model from determining connections that are very common to a specific decision tree. In other words, higher values can be used to constrain the decision tree.

2. min samples leaf: This is the parameter you need to adjust to determine how many observations a node, or leaf, requires. The overfitting control mechanism functions in the same way that the sample split parameter does.

3. max features: Modify this parameter to control the features that are chosen at random. These are the characteristics that are used to perform the best split. Calculate the square root of the total features to find the most efficient value. Just keep in mind that in this case, the higher value tends to exacerbate the overfitting problem we're attempting to address. As a result, you should experiment with the value you choose. Furthermore, not every case is the same. A higher value will sometimes work without causing overfitting.

4. max-depth: Finally, we have the depth parameter, which consists of the decision tree's depth value. However, in order to limit the overfitting problem, we are only interested in the maximum depth value. Keep in mind that a high value corresponds to a high number of splits, and thus a high amount of information. You can control how the training model learns the connections in a sample by adjusting this value.

Changing these parameters is only one aspect of gaining control over our decision trees in order to reduce overfitting and improve performance and accuracy. Following the application of these constraints, the trees must be pruned.

Pruning

This technique may appear to be too absurd to be true; however, it is a legitimate machine learning concept that is used to improve your decision tree by nearly eliminating overfitting. Pruning, like real tree pruning, reduces the size of the trees in order to focus resources on providing highly accurate results. However, you should keep in mind that the pruned segments are not chosen at random, which is a good thing. Sections that are removed are those that do not aid in classification and do not result in any performance improvements. Less complex decision trees result in a more optimised model.

Visualize the following scenario to better understand the difference between an unmodified decision tree and one that has been pruned and optimised. Assume there is a highway with one lane for vehicles travelling at 80 mph and another lane for slower vehicles travelling at 50 mph. Assume you're driving down the highway in a red car and you're faced with a decision. You have the option of moving to the fast lane to pass a slow-moving car; however, this means that you will have a truck in front of you who is unable to achieve the high speed he should in the left lane, and thus you will be stuck in that lane. In this case, the cars in the other lane are gradually overtaking you because the truck is unable to keep up. The other option is to stay in your lane and not try to overtake. The best option here is one that allows you to travel a longer distance in a shorter amount of time.

As a result, if you stay in the slow lane until you gradually pass the truck blocking the fast lane, you will eventually be able to switch to that lane and pass all of the other vehicles. As you can see, the second option appears to be the slowest at the time of consideration; however, in the long run, it is the most efficient.

The decision trees are all the same. When you set limits for your trees, they will not become greedy and switch you to the left lane, where you will be stuck behind a truck. However, pruning the decision tree will allow you to examine your surroundings in greater detail and predict a greater number of options you have to make a better choice.

As you can see, performing the pruning process has some significant advantages that should not be overlooked. However, putting this technique into action necessitates a number of steps and conditions. A decision tree, for example, must have a high depth value in order to be suitable for pruning. Furthermore, in order to avoid negative outcomes, the process must begin at the bottom. This problem must be avoided because if a negative node split occurs at the bottom and another at the top, we will end up with a decision tree that stops when the first division occurs. If the tree is pruned, it will continue to grow, resulting in greater profits.

When all you have is a theory, it can be difficult to visualise decision trees, so let's start with a step-by-step implementation to see them in action.

Implementation of a Decision Tree

Making a decision tree begins with the root node. The first step is to choose one of the data attributes and create a logical test around it.

Once you have a set of results, you can branch out and write another set of tests to create the subnode. Once we have at least one subnode, we can use a recursive splitting process to determine whether or not we have clean decision tree leaves. Keep in mind that the purity level is determined by the number of cases that arise from a single class. At this point, you can begin pruning the tree to remove anything that does not improve the classification stage's accuracy. You will also need to evaluate each and every split that is performed based on each attribute. This step must be completed in order to determine which attribute, as well as split, is the most optimal.

But that's enough theory for now. At this point, all you should be concerned with is the fundamental concept of decision trees and how to make them efficient. Once you believe you have a firm grasp on the fundamentals, you must begin the implementation process.

In the following example, we will once again rely on the Iris dataset and the Scikit-learn library to provide the data.

K-means Clustering

Unsupervised learning methods, as previously stated, are ideal for working with unlabeled data. To be more specific, one of the best, if not the best, technique is to use a type of clustering algorithm.

The cluster analysis is the main idea behind this approach, which involves reducing data observations to clusters, or subdivisions of data, where each cluster contains information that is similar to that of a predefined attribute. Clustering entails a number of techniques that all work toward the same goal because they are all concerned with developing a variety of theories about the data structure.

K-means clustering is one of the most widely used unsupervised learning algorithms and clustering techniques. The idea behind this concept is to create data clusters based on the similarity of the values. The first step is to calculate k, which is represented by the total number of clusters we define. These clusters are made up of k-many points, each of which contains the average value for the entire cluster. Furthermore, the values are assigned based on the closest average value. Remember that clusters have a core, which is defined as an average value that pushes the other averages aside, causing them to change. After a sufficient number of iterations, the core value will shift to a lower performance metric. We have the solutions when we reach this stage because there are no observations available to be designated.

It's okay if all of this theory has left you perplexed. You'll notice that this technique is much simpler than it appears. Let's take a look at how it's done in practise. We'll use the UCI handwritten digits dataset in this example. It's free, and you don't need to download it if you're using Scikit-learn in conjunction with the book. With that said, here is the code:

```
import time import numpy as np import
matplotlib.pyplot as plt import datasets from
sklearn import datasets

np.random.seed()

datasets.load digits() digits = datasets.data
scale(digits.data) n samples, n features =
data.shape

len(np.unique(digits.target)) n digits =
len(np.unique(digits.target))

labels = digits. sample size target = 300

print

("n digits:% d, t n samples:% d, t n features:% d")
percent (n digits, n samples, n features))

print(79 * '_') print('percent 9s' percent 'init" time
inertia homo compl v-meas ARI AMI silhouette')
print('percent 9s' percent 'init" time inertia homo
compl v-meas ARI AMI silhouette')

bench k means(estimator, name, and data):

t0 denotes time ()

estimator.fit(data) \sprint
```

(' percent 9s percent.2fs percent | percent.3f percent.3f percent.3f percent.3f percent.3f percent.3f percent.3f percent.3f percent.3f percent.3f percent.3f percent.3f percent.3f percent.3f percent.3f' percent (name, (time() - t0), estimator.inertia_, metrics.homogeneity score(labels, estimator.labels_), metrics.completeness score(labels, estimator.labels_), metrics.v measure score(labels, estimator.labels_), metrics.adjusted rand score(labels, estimator.labels_), metrics.silhouette score(data, estimator. Adapted from https://techwithtim.net/tutorials/machine-learning-Python/kmeans-2/ (last visited in October 2019)

If you examine the code line by line, you will notice that the implementation is relatively simple, logical, and simple to grasp. In fact, it is similar in some ways to other techniques we have used previously. However, there is one significant difference to note, and that is the performance measurements we use to accurately interpret the data.

First, we have a score for homogeneity. This metric can have a value ranging from 0 to 1. It is primarily interested in clusters that have only one class system. The idea is that if we have a score that is close to one, then the cluster is mostly made up of samples from a single class. If, on the other hand, the score is close to zero, we have achieved a low level of homogeneity.

The completeness score comes next. This metric supplements the measure of homogeneity. Its purpose is to inform us about how the measurements became a part of a specific class. The two scores allow us to conclude that we either performed perfect clustering or we simply failed.

The third metric is known as the V-metric or, more colloquially, the Vmeasure. The harmonic mean of the previous two scores is used to calculate this score. The V-metric essentially verifies the validity by assigning a zero to one value to the homogeneity and completeness score.

The adjusted Rand index metric comes next. This is a score that is used to verify the labeling's similarity. The Rand index simply determines the relationship between the distribution sets by using a value between zero and one.

Finally, the silhouette metric is used to determine whether the performance of the clustering is adequate in the absence of labelled data. The measurement ranges from a negative to a positive value and determines whether or not the clusters are well-structured. If the value is negative, we have a problem with bad clusters. To ensure dense clusters, we must achieve a score close to a positive one. Remember that in this case, we could also have a score close to zero. In this case, the silhouette measurement indicates that we have clusters that overlap.

Now that you understand the measurement system, we need to take one more step to ensure that the results are accurate. We can use the bench k means function to validate the clustering scores as follows:

bench k means(KMeans(init='k-means++', n clusters=n digits, n init=10), name="k-means++," data=data) print(79 * ' ')

Let's see what we can deduce from the scores now. Here's an example of how your results should look:

n samples 1797 n features n digits 10 Inertia of 64 init time homogeneous

init v-meas k-means++ 0.25s 69517 0.596 0.643 The silhouette of ARI AMI

0.619 0.465 0.592 0.123 k-means++

As you can see, we have fairly good results with a basic k-means implementation; however, there is much room for improvement. Although clustering is sufficient, we could improve the scores by implementing other supervised or unsupervised learning techniques. In this case, for example, you might think about using the principal component analysis algorithm as well. Another option is to use various dimensionality reduction methods. These results, however, will suffice to learn how to implement the K-means clustering algorithm. However, keep in mind that in the real world of Data Science, you will frequently combine several algorithms and techniques. You will almost never be able to get useful results with just one algorithm, especially if you are working with raw datasets rather than practise ones.

In this chapter, we learned about unsupervised learning algorithms, specifically K-means clustering. The goal of this section was to demonstrate a technique that can be applied to more complex datasets. Clustering algorithms are a Data Science staple and are frequently used, particularly in conjunction with other algorithms and learning techniques. Furthermore, as you will discover later, clustering techniques, particularly K-means clustering, are extremely effective in dealing with Big Data.

Chapter 9: Real World Applications

The use of Big Data and Big Data Analytics benefits both small and large businesses in a variety of industrial domains. In this chapter, we will delve deeper into such applications.

eCommerce

Customers and potential customers for every company are among the over 2.6 billion active social media users. The race is on to develop more effective marketing and social media strategies powered by machine learning, with the goal of providing an improved customer experience and converting prospective customers into raving fans. Sifting through and analysing massive amounts of data has not only become feasible but also simple. Artificial intelligence marketing solutions have helped to bridge the gap between execution and big data analysis.

Artificial Intelligence (AI) marketing is a method of using artificial intelligence consonants such as machine learning on available customer data to anticipate customer needs and expectations while significantly improving the customer journey.

Marketers can improve campaign performance and ROI with little to no extra effort thanks to big data insights provided by artificial intelligence marketing solutions. The following are the key elements that contribute to the effectiveness of AI marketing:

Big data - The ability of a marketing firm to aggregate and segment a massive dump of data with minimal manual work is referred to as Big Data. The marketer can then use the appropriate medium to ensure that the appropriate message is delivered to the target audience at the appropriate time.

Machine learning platforms enable marketers to identify trends or common occurrences and gather effective insights and responses, allowing them to decipher the root cause and probability of recurring events.

Intuitive platform – AI marketing relies on applications that are both fast and simple to use. Artificial intelligence technology can interpret emotions and communicate like a human, allowing

AI-powered platforms to understand open form content such as email responses and social media.

Predictive Modeling

All solutions based on artificial intelligence technology are capable of extracting information from data assets in order to forecast future trends. AI technology has enabled the modelling of trends that could previously only be determined retroactively. These predictive analysis models can be used to make sound decisions and analyse customer purchasing behaviour. The model can successfully predict when a consumer is more likely to make a new purchase or reorder an old one. Marketing firms can now reverse engineer their customers' experiences and actions to develop more profitable marketing strategies. FedEx and Sprint, for example, use predictive analytics to identify customers who are at risk of defecting to a competitor.

Intelligent searches

Only a decade ago, if you typed in "women's flip flops" on Nike.com, the chances of finding what you were looking for were almost nil. Today's search engines, on the other hand, are not only

111

more accurate but also much faster. This advancement has been largely driven by advancements such as "semantic search" and "natural language processing," which allow search engines to identify links between products and provide relevant search results, recommend similar items, and auto-correct typing errors. Artificial intelligence and big data solutions can quickly analyse user search patterns and identify key areas where marketing firms should focus their efforts.

Google launched the first Artificial Intelligence-based search algorithm, "RankBrain," in 2015. Following in Google's footsteps, other major e-commerce websites, such as Amazon, have incorporated Big Data Analysis and artificial intelligence into their search engines to provide smart search experiences for their customers, allowing them to find desired products even when they don't know exactly what they're looking for. Smart search technologies such as "Elasticsearch" are available to even small e-commerce stores. Companies that provide data as a service, such as "Indix," "allow businesses to train their product search models using data from other larger data sources

Engines of Recommendation

Recommendation engines have quickly become fan favourites, and customers adore them just as much as marketing firms. "Apple Music" already knows your music preferences better than your partner, and Amazon always shows you a list of products you might be interested in purchasing. This type of discovery tool, which can sift through millions of available options and zero in on an individual's needs, is proving invaluable for large corporations with massive physical and digital inventories.

Jussi Karlgren, a Swedish computational linguist, investigated the practise of clustering customer behaviours to predict future behaviours in his report titled "Digital bookshelves" in 1998. Amazon implemented collaborative filtering the same year to generate recommendations for their customers. The predictive analysis-based systems gather and analyse consumer data, along with individual profile information and demographics, allowing the system to continually learn and adapt based on consumer activities such as likes and dislikes on products in real-time. For example, "Sky" has implemented a predictive analysis-based model capable of recommending content based on the viewer's mode.

The savvy consumer expects such an improved experience not only from their music and on-demand entertainment providers but also from all other e-commerce websites.

Pricing and Product Categorization

E-commerce companies and marketing firms are increasingly incorporating artificial intelligence into their inventory categorization and tagging processes. Marketing firms must deal with bad data just as much, if not more than they do with well-organized, clean data. This collection of positive and negative examples is used to train predictive analysis-based classification tools. For example, different retailers may use different descriptions for the same product, such as sneakers, basketball shoes, trainers, or Jordans, but the AI algorithm can recognise that these are all the same products and tag them appropriately. If the data set lacks the primary keyword, such as skirts or shirts, the artificial intelligence algorithm can identify and classify the item or product as skirts or shirts based solely on the surrounding context.

Hotel room rates change seasonally, but with the advent of artificial intelligence, product prices can be optimised to meet demand with a whole new level of precision.

Machine learning algorithms are used for dynamic pricing by analysing customer data patterns and making near-accurate predictions of what they are willing to pay for that specific product as well as their receptivity to special offers. This enables businesses to precisely target their consumers and determine whether or not a discount is required to complete the sale.

Dynamic pricing also enables businesses to compare their product pricing with market leaders and competitors, and then adjust their prices to close the sale. For example, "AirbnB" has created a dynamic pricing system that provides property owners with "Price Tips" to help them determine the best possible listing price for their property. The system considers a number of influencing factors, including geographical location, local events, property photos, property reviews, listing features, and, most importantly, booking timings and market demand. The system will also monitor the property owner's final decision to follow or ignore the provided 'price tips,' as well as the success of the listing, and will then process the results and adjust its algorithm accordingly.

Customer segmentation and targeting

Marketing firms must target increasingly granular segments in order to reach their customers with a high level of personalization. Machine learning algorithms can be trained against "gold standard" training sets using existing customer data to identify common properties and significant variables. Data segments could be as simple as location, gender, and age, or as complex as the buyer's persona and previous behaviour. Segmentation is possible with AI Dynamics, which accounts for the fact that customers' behaviours change all the time and that people can take on different people in different situations.

Forecast for Sales and Marketing

The development of sales and marketing forecasting models is one of the most straightforward artificial intelligence applications in marketing. The machine learning algorithms use a large amount of quantifiable data, such as clicks, purchases, email responses, and time spent on webpages, as training resources. Sisense, Rapidminer, and Birst are three of the market's leading business intelligence and production companies. Marketing firms are constantly improving their marketing efforts, and they can predict the success of their marketing initiatives or email campaigns using AI and machine learning. Artificial intelligence technology can predict short and long-term sales performance and forecast sales outcomes by analysing past sales data, economic trends, and industrywide comparisons. The sales forecasting model assists in estimating product demand and assisting businesses in managing production to maximise sales.

Targeting of Programmatic Ads

Bidding on and targeting program-based advertisements has become significantly more efficient since the introduction of artificial intelligence technology. The automated process of buying and selling ad inventory to an exchange that connects advertisers and publishers is known as programmatic advertising. Artificial intelligence technology is used to enable real-time bidding for inventory across social media channels, mobile devices, and television. This also relates to predictive analytics and the ability to model data that was previously only determined retrospectively.

Artificial intelligence can help determine the best time of day to serve a specific ad, the likelihood of an ad converting into sales, the user's receptiveness, and the likelihood of engagement with the ad.

Programmatic companies can collect and analyse data and behaviours from visiting customers in order to optimise real-time campaigns and target the audience more precisely. The use of "demand-side platforms" (to facilitate the process of buying ad inventory on the open market) and "data management platforms" (to provide the marketing company with the ability to reach their target audience) is included in programmatic media buying. The data management platforms are designed to collect and analyse a large volume of website "cookie data" in order to empower marketing representatives to make informed decisions about their prospective customers. Channels such as Facebook, Twitter, and Google, for example, use search engine marketing (SEM) advertising. Programmatic ads provide a significant advantage over competitors in terms of efficiently managing a large inventory of website and application viewers. Google and Facebook are the gold standard for efficient and effective advertising, with a user-friendly platform that allows nontechnical marketing companies to start, run, and measure their initiatives and campaigns online.

Image Recognition and Visual Search

Artificial intelligence-based image recognition and analysis technology has advanced by leaps and bounds, resulting in uncanny visual search functionalities. With the introduction of technology such as Google Lens and platforms such as Pinterest, people can now use visual search functionality to find results that are visually similar to one another. The visual search function is similar to traditional text-based searches in that it returns results on a similar topic.

Major retailers and marketing firms are increasingly utilising visual search to provide a more enhanced and engaging customer experience. Instead of the consumer's previous behaviour or purchases, visual search can be used to improve merchandising and provide product recommendations based on the style of the product.

Target and Asos have made significant investments in the development of visual search technology for their e-commerce websites. Target announced a partnership with Pinterest in 2017 that allows for the integration of Pinterest's visual search application, known as "Pinterest lens," into Target's mobile application. As a result, shoppers can take pictures of products they want to buy while out and about and find similar items on Target's e-commerce site.

Similarly, Asos' "Asos' Style Match" visual search application allows shoppers to snap a photo or upload an image on the Asos website or application and search their product catalogue for similar items. These tools entice shoppers to visit retailers for items they may have seen in a magazine or while out and about by assisting them in shopping for the ideal product even if they do not know what the product is.

Image recognition has greatly aided marketers in getting a head start on social media by allowing them to find a variety of uses for their brands' logos and products in order to stay current with visual trends. This phenomenon, also known as "visual social listening," enables businesses to identify and understand where and how customers interact with their brand, logo, and product even when the company is not directly referred to by its name.

Industry of Healthcare

Big Data Analysis has resulted in a paradigm shift in healthcare due to the increasing availability of healthcare data. The analysis of relationships between patient outcomes and the treatment or prevention technique used is the primary focus of big data analytics in the healthcare industry. Big Data Analysis-driven Artificial Intelligence programmes for patient diagnostics, treatment protocol generation, drug development, and patient monitoring and care have all been developed successfully. The advanced AI techniques can sift through massive amounts of clinical data and help unlock clinically relevant information to aid decision making.

Some medical specialties that are seeing an increase in Big Data Analysis-based AI research and applications include:

Radiology – AI's ability to interpret imaging results supplements the clinician's ability to detect changes in an image that the human eye can easily miss. An artificial intelligence algorithm developed recently at Stanford University can detect specific sites in the lungs of pneumonia patients.

Electronic Health Records – The requirement for digital health records in order to optimise information dissemination and access necessitates the rapid and accurate logging of all health-related data in the systems. Humans are prone to errors and can suffer from cognitive overload and burnout. AI has successfully automated this process.

At baseline, the use of predictive models on electronic health record data allowed for the prediction of individualised treatment response with 70-72 percent accuracy.

Imaging – Ongoing AI research is assisting doctors in assessing the outcome of corrective jaw surgery as well as cleft palate therapy to predict facial attractiveness.

Industry of Entertainment

Big Data Analysis, in collaboration with Artificial Intelligence, is increasingly running in the background of entertainment sources ranging from video games to movies, providing us with a richer, more engaging, and realistic experience. Big Data Analysis is being used by entertainment providers such as Netflix and Hulu to provide users with personalised recommendations based on their historical activity and behaviour. Big Data Analysis-based tools have been used by computer graphics and digital media content producers to improve the speed and efficiency of their production processes. Machine learning algorithms are increasingly being used by film studios in the creation of film trailers and advertisements, as well as in pre- and post-production processes. For example, big data analysis and an artificial intelligence-powered tool called "RivetAI" enable producers to automate and read the processes of movie script breakdown, storyboard, budgeting, scheduling, and shot-list generation. Certain time-consuming tasks performed during film post-production, such as synchronisation and clip assembly, can be easily automated using artificial intelligence.

Advertising and marketing

A machine learning algorithm created as a result of big data analysis can be easily trained using text, still images, and video segments as data sources. It can then extract objects and concepts from these sources and make recommendations for effective marketing and advertising solutions. As an example, consider the tool "Alibaba created "Luban," which can create banners at a much faster rate than a human designer. Luban generated 117 million banner designs in 2016 for the Chinese online shopping extravaganza known as "Singles Day" at a rate of 8000 banner designs per second.

20th Century Fox collaborated with IBM to create the trailer for their horror film "Morgan" using their AI system "Watson."

Watson was trained to classify and analyse input "moments" from audio-visual and other composition elements from over a hundred horror movies in order to learn the appropriate "moments" or clips that should appear in a standard horror movie trailer. Watson used this training to create a six-minute movie trailer in just 24 hours, which would have taken a human professional weeks to create.

An AI marketing platform can accelerate the marketing process exponentially by utilising Machine Learning, computer vision technology, natural language processing, and predictive analytics. Albert Intelligence Marketing's artificial intelligence-based marketing platform, for example, can generate autonomous campaign management strategies, create custom solutions, and perform audience targeting. The use of their AI-based platform resulted in an 183 percent increase in customer transaction rate and a 600 percent increase in conversation efficiency, according to the company.

McCann Erickson Japan introduced the "AI-CD ß" artificial intelligence-based creative director in March 2016 as the world's first robotic creative director. "AI-CD ß" "was trained on specific elements of various TV shows, as well as the winners of the All Japan Radio and Television CM festival for the previous ten years.

Data mining capabilities can be used to "AI-CD ß" can extract ideas and themes that are tailored to each client's specific campaign requirements.

User Experience Personalization

On-demand entertainment users' expectations for a rich and engaging personal user experience are constantly rising. Netflix, one of the leading on-demand entertainment platforms, has released "Meson," an artificial intelligence-based workflow management and scheduling application comprised of various "machine learning pipelines" capable of creating, training, and validating personalization algorithms to provide personalised recommendations to users. Netflix collaborated with the University of Southern California to create

"Dynamic Optimizer," a new Machine Learning algorithm that can compress video for high-quality streaming without sacrificing image quality. By optimising video fluency and definition, this artificial intelligence technology will address streaming issues in developing countries and among mobile device users.

IBM Watson recently partnered with IRIS.TV to provide a business-to-business service to media companies such as CBS, The Hollywood Reporter, and Hearst Digital Media by tracking and improving customer introductions to web content.

IBM Watson is enhancing IRIS.TV's machine learning algorithms, which can 'learn' from users' search histories and recommend similar content. According to reports, the Hollywood reporter achieved a 50 percent increase in view or retention of a small PDF three months after using the IRIS.TV application.

Classification and Search Optimization

The ability to digitise text, audio, and video content has resulted in an explosion of media availability on the Internet, making it difficult for people to find exactly what they're looking for.

Machine learning technology is being improved to improve the accuracy of search results. Google, for example, is incorporating artificial intelligence into its platform to improve image search accuracy. Instead of typing in keywords for their search, people can now simply upload a sample image to Google Image. Google Image's image recognition technology will automatically identify and manage features of the uploaded user image and return search results with similar images. Google also employs artificial intelligence technology in ad placement across the platform. A pet food advertisement, for example, will only appear on a pet-related website, whereas a chicken wings advertisement will not appear on a vegetarian-targeted website.

Vintage Cloud has collaborated with an artificial intelligence-based startup called " "larifAI" to create a platform for film digitalization. Vintage Cloud was able to increase the speed of movie content classification and categorization by utilising ClarifAI's computer vision API.

A company called "Zorroa" has created a visual asset management platform that is integrated with machine learning algorithms " This platform, known as a "Analysis Pipeline," allows users to search for specific content within large databases. The database contains processors that can uniquely tag each visual asset as well as machine learning algorithms that have been 'trained' to recognise specific components of the visual data. This visual content is then organised and catalogued so that high-quality search results can be delivered.

Chapter 10: Data in the Cloud

Data Science is a mash-up of many ideas. It is necessary to have some programming skills in order to become a data scientist. Even if you do not understand all of the programming concepts related to infrastructure, having a basic understanding of computer science concepts is required. On your computer, you must install the two most popular and widely used programming languages, R and Python. With the ever-expanding capabilities of advanced analytics, Data Science is spreading its wings in new directions. This necessitates the use of collaborative solutions such as predictive analysis and recommendation systems. Research and notebook tools integrated with code source control are examples of collaboration solutions. Data Science is also associated with the cloud. The data is also saved in the cloud. As a result, this lesson will enlighten you on some facts about "data in the Cloud." So, first, let's define the term "cloud," as well as how data is stored and how it works.

What exactly is the Cloud?

The cloud can be defined as a global server network with distinct functions. Understanding networks is required for cloud research. Networks can be simple or complex information or data clusters.

Network

As previously stated, networks can connect a simple or small group of computers or large groups of computers. The Internet has the potential to be the largest network. Small groups can be home local networks, such as Wi-Fi, or Local Area Networks that are restricted to specific computers or locations. Shared networks include media, web pages, app servers, data storage, printers, and scanners. Nodes are components of networks, and a computer is an example of a node. Protocols are used to establish communication between these computers. Protocols are the computer's intermediary rules. Protocols such as HTTP, TCP, and IP are widely used. Although all of the information is stored on the computer, it becomes difficult to search for information on the computer each time. Typically, such data is kept in a Data Center. A Data Centre is built in such a way that it provides support security and data protection.

Since the cost of computers and storage has decreased significantly, many organisations prefer to use multiple computers that work together when scaling. This is distinct from other scaling solutions, such as purchasing additional computing devices. The goal is to keep the work going even if one of the computers fails; the other will continue the operation. Some cloud applications must be scaled as well.

Taking a broad look at some computing applications that require scaling, such as YouTube, Netflix, and Facebook. We rarely see such applications fail because their systems are hosted in the cloud. In the cloud, there is a network cluster where many computers are connected to the same networks and perform similar tasks. It can be referred to as a single source of information or a single computer that manages everything in order to improve performance, scalability, and availability.

Cloud-based Data Science

The entire Data Science process takes place on the local machine, which is a computer or laptop provided to the data scientist. The computer or laptop has pre-installed programming languages as well as a few other requirements. Common programming languages and algorithms are examples of this. The data scientist must then install the necessary software and development packages for his or her project. Anaconda and other similar managers can be used to install development packages. You can also choose to install them manually. Once you have installed and entered the development environment, your first step, i.e., the workflow, will begin where your companion is only data. It is not required to perform Data Science or Big Data tasks on different development machines. Consider the following reasons:

1. The processing time required to complete tasks on the development environment fails due to a lack of processing power.

2. The presence of large data sets that cannot be stored in the system memory of the development environment.

3. Deliverables must be assembled in a production environment and integrated as a component in a large application.

4. It is recommended that you use a machine that is both fast and powerful.

When confronted with such problems, data scientists consider a variety of options, including on-premise machines and virtual machines that run in the cloud. Using virtual machines and auto-scaling clusters has several advantages, including the ability to scale up and down as needed. Virtual machines are configured to meet a user's computing power and storage requirements. Deploying the information in a production environment to push it through a large data pipeline may present some challenges. The data scientist must comprehend and analyse these challenges. This is understandable if you have a basic understanding of software architectures and quality attributes.

Quality Attributes and Software Architecture

Software Architects create a cloud-based software system.

Such systems could be a product or service that is reliant on a computing system. When developing software, the primary task is to choose the appropriate programming language to be used. The system's purpose may be called into question; therefore, it must be taken into account. Developing and working with software architecture requires a highly skilled individual. The majority of organisations have begun to implement an effective and dependable cloud environment through the use of cloud computing. These cloud environments are distributed across a variety of servers, storage, and networking resources. This is widely used due to its low cost and high ROI.

The main advantage for data scientists or their teams is that they can use the large amount of space in the cloud to explore more data and develop important use cases. You can release a feature and have it tested the next second to see if it adds value or if it isn't worth carrying forward. All of this immediate action is made possible by cloud computing.

Cloud-based Big Data Sharing

Big Data plays an important role when dealing with the cloud because it makes it easier to track and analyse insights. Once this is established, big data provides significant value to users.

The conventional method was to process wired data. With this technique, it became difficult for the team to share their information. The usual issues included large amounts of data transfer and data collaboration. This is where cloud computing began to germinate in the competitive world.

Because of cloud computing, all of these issues were eliminated, and teams were gradually able to collaborate from different locations, including overseas.

As a result, cloud computing is critical in both Data Science and Big Data. The cloud is used by the majority of organisations. Swiggy, Uber, Airbnb, and other companies that use the cloud are examples. They make use of cloud computing to share information and data.

Governance of Cloud and Big Data

Working with the cloud is a fantastic experience because it reduces resource costs, time, and manual labour. However, the question of how organisations deal with security, compliance, and governance arises.

Most businesses find it difficult to comply with such regulations. Working with the cloud has issues related to privacy and security that are not limited to Big Data. As a result, developing a strong governance policy for your cloud solutions is essential. You must maintain an open architecture to ensure that your cloud solutions are reliable, robust, and governable.

Data is required. Cloud Tools for Delivering High-Value Data

In this day and age, there is a high demand for data scientists. They are in charge of assisting large and small organisations in developing useful information from the provided data or data set. Large organisations have a lot of data that needs to be analysed all the time.

According to recent reports, nearly 80% of unstructured data received by organisations is in the form of social media, emails (e.g., Outlook, Gmail, etc.), videos, images, and so on. With the rapid growth of cloud computing, data scientists are dealing with a plethora of new workloads resulting from IoT, AI, Blockchain, Analytics, and so on. Working with all of these new workloads necessitates a stable, efficient, and centralised platform that can be shared by all teams. All of this necessitates the management and recording of new data as well as legacy documents.

Once a data scientist is assigned a task and given a dataset to work with, he or she must have the necessary skills to analyse the ever-increasing volumes using cloud technologies. They must transform the data into useful insights that will be responsible for growing the business. The data scientist must create an algorithm as well as code the programme. They spend roughly 80% of their time gathering information, creating and modifying data, cleaning as needed, and organising data. The remaining 20% is used for data analysis through effective programming. This necessitates the use of specific cloud tools to assist data scientists in saving time when searching for relevant information. Organizations should make new cloud services and cloud tools available to their respective data scientists so that they can quickly organise massive amounts of data. As a result, cloud tools are critical for a data scientist to analyse large amounts of data in a short period of time. It will save the company time and aid in the development of strong and robust Data Models.

Chapter 11: Conclusion

Thank you for persevering until the end! The next step is to get started by determining how Data Science can benefit your company. You will discover that there are numerous applications for the vast amount of information that you have at your disposal, as well as all of the data that you have accumulated over time. Data collection is only the first step in the process. We also need to ensure that we can gain all of the insights and predictions that come from that information, which is where the Data Science process comes into play.

This guidebook has taken the time to investigate what Data Science is all about and how it can benefit your company in a variety of ways. We discussed some of the tasks that Data Science can assist with, what Data Science is and how to work with the data life cycle, the future of data, and much more. This allows us to see some of the components of data analysis, as well as how beneficial gathering and utilising all of that information can be to the growth of your business.

However, this is not the only step we can take. We also need to go a step further and be able to analyse the data to see what information it contains, rather than just collecting it. This is a part of the Data Science life cycle, but it deserves special attention because, without it, the data would simply sit there unutilized.

In this guidebook, we looked at the Python coding language and how it could help us work through all of that data, collecting models and more, so we could learn something and make predictions about it. This guidebook spent some time introducing Python and how it works before moving on to some of the best libraries that you can use to not only write codes in Python but also to work on various models for analysing the data you have.

Data Science is a great addition to your business because it can help you ensure that customer satisfaction is high, waste is low, you can make more money, and it can even help with future predictions, such as what products you should develop and put on the market. Learning all of this, however, does not happen by itself. Working with Data Science and incorporating some Python language and the various libraries that come with it can make a big difference. When you're ready to use Python Data Science to improve many different aspects of your business and beat the competition, make sure to revisit this guidebook to help you get started right away.

Lightning Source UK Ltd.
Milton Keynes UK
UKHW022308070223
416656UK00014B/163